T.L. OSBORN

TRAGEDY TRAUMA TRIUMPH

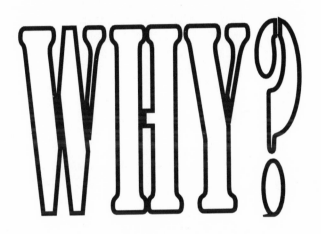

i

INTERNATIONAL DISTRIBUTOR
of Osborn Books.
ACCESS INTERNATIONAL
P.O. Box 700143,
Tulsa, OK 74170-0143 USA

✧✧✧

FRENCH DISTRIBUTORS
Assoc. IMPACT PLEIN EVANGILE
32140 Panassac, France

◻ ◻ ◻

VIE ABONDANTE, B.P. 241,
03208 Vichy, Cedex France

✧✧✧

GERMAN PUBLISHER
SHALOM — VERLAG
Pachlinger Strrasse 10
D-93486 Runding, CHAM, Germany

✧✧✧

PORTUGUESE PUBLISHER
GRACA EDITORIAL
Caixa Postal 1815
Rio de Janiero–RJ–20001, Brazil

✧✧✧

SPANISH PUBLISHER
LIBROS DESAFIO, Apdo. 29724
Bogota, Colombia

✧✧✧

(For Quantity Orders, Request Discount Prices.)

BOOKS BY
T.L. AND DAISY OSBORN

FIVE CHOICES FOR WOMEN WHO WIN
GOD'S LOVE PLAN
HEALING THE SICK – A Living Classic
HOW TO BE BORN AGAIN
NEW LIFE FOR WOMEN
POWER OF POSITIVE DESIRE
RECEIVE MIRACLE HEALING
SOULWINNING - A Classic on Evangelism
THE BEST OF LIFE
THE GOOD LIFE
THE GOSPEL, ACCORDING TO T.L. & DAISY
THE WOMAN BELIEVER
THE MESSAGE THAT WORKS
WHY? Tragedy Trauma Triumph
WOMAN WITHOUT LIMITS
WOMEN & SELF-ESTEEM
YOU ARE GOD'S BEST

For these and other titles, contact:
⬛S🅵⬛ Publishers
P.O. Box 10, Tulsa, OK 74102 USA
Tel: 918 743 6231
Fax: 918 749 0339 E-Mail: OSFO@aol.com

Canada: Box 281, Adelaide St. Post Sta.,
Toronto M5C 2J4
England: Box 148, Birmingham B3 2LG

BIBLE QUOTATIONS in this book are derived from the King James Version unless otherwise noted. (References are included.) They are sometimes personalized, paraphrased or abridged to facilitate clarity and to encourage individual application. We have taken the liberty of conforming them, in structure, to the person and tense of their contextual application.

The Author

Table of Contents

In Memory Of:

My wonderful and loving wife
for almost fifty-four years,

My patient companion and teammate
in the Lord's work
from the date of our marriage
on April 5, 1942,

My trusted colleague and associate
in mass miracle evangelism
in seventy-four nations of the world,

My courageous and untiring co-worker
in God's No. 1 Job of ministering
Love in our hurting world,

My special confidant and counselor
in every phase and outreach of
our world ministries to millions,

My most cherished and loving friend,

My intimate and faithful sweetheart, and

The one and only Special Lady in my life,

Daisy Marie Washburn Osborn

"*I am a voice announcing that your Redemption has come, that your Redeemer is here, that your Emancipation has been declared, that your Ransom is paid; and I am announcing it boldly to women and men of all races and colors.*"-Dr. Daisy Marie Washburn Osborn

T.L. Osborn walks alone from the funeral limousine to Daisy's burying-place for the graveside ceremony and final committal of his beloved wife back to God.

After Daisy's Demise

*This chronicle was conceived
during our conferences
in the ex-Soviet Union republics.*

♦ BEGAN THESE ANNALS AT *MURMANSK*,
RUSSIA, ABOVE THE ARCTIC CIRCLE;

♦ CONTINUED LOGGING THESE EVENTS
AT *MINSK*, BELARUS;

♦ PROGRESSED WITH NOTING OCCURRENCES
AT *ALMA ATA*, KAZHAKSTAN;

♦ OUTLINED THE EVENTS OF THE PAST YEAR
IN *BISHKEK*, KHRGYZSTAN;

♦ BEGAN WRITING THESE MEMOIRS
AT *NOVOSIBIRSK*, SIBERIA, RUSSIA;

♦ CONTINUED CHRONICLING THE EVENTS
AT *PERM*, IN THE URALS, RUSSIA;

♦ PROCEEDED WITH JOURNAL OF REMINISCENCES
AT *KHARKOV*, UKRAINE;

♦ FINISHED CATALOGING AND RECORDING
THESE LESSONS AND RECOLLECTIONS
AT *MOSCOW*, RUSSIA, *UPPSALA*, SWEDEN, *THIRSK*,
ENGLAND, *HELSINKI*, FINLAND,
BANGKOK, THAILAND, *OSLO*, NORWAY,
MEDELLIN, COLOMBIA AND
IN MY LIBRARY-STUDY AT TULSA, OK, USA.

Introduction

Untapping New Resources

I'VE DECIDED TO SHARE some significant experiences that have transpired since the demise of my beloved wife, Daisy. This chronicle is too personal to publish, except for the fact that tragedy and loss are universal, and a significant part of life is learning to grow through adversity.

The greatest possible trauma is to lose faith and hope. If those flames are extinguished, then one is dead although his or her heart still beats.

The pathos of chaos can strike in unexpected ways and at unpredictable times. Calamitous loss may result from death, flood, fire, storm, divorce, or as a result of many other traumatic events. Anguish and sorrow can be overwhelming.

I have wrestled with my emotions, searching to discover who is this man, T.L. Osborn. I know who T.L. & Daisy are. But T.L.—alone, by himself—I am having to get acquainted with him.

Taking Command

Amidst the grief and agony of loss, memory plays a significant role. At each onslaught of emptiness, I have learned to take command of my emotions, to analyze what and where the pain is, then to examine my feelings and to guard my mental equilibrium. I query, "Am I indulging in *self-pity?* Is there real pain within my body? If so, where is it? What is causing it?"

Then, always, I return to the premise: *Distress is induced by one's own thoughts. We have the power to alter our thinking.*

I do not want my memories of Daisy to dissipate. Reflection on our lives and love together is a treasury for me. But I must view my memories with a new perspective—with *gratitude* and not with *remorse.* I must embrace the facts of life and discover the beauty of my altered vista.

Reconciling With Change

I have never before lived alone. So I must learn to value life and to function—*without Daisy,* accepting the fact that *her* earthly life has ended.

Her physical presence is no longer mine to touch. Her brilliant mind, her counsel, her wisdom are no longer accessible to me. I must be reconciled with life *as it now is for me.* My life as a married man has ended. I must face that.

Delight Rather Than Distress

I must modify my thinking and re-ponder my memories of Daisy with *delight*, rather than with *remorse*. The years together with her are full of priceless memories that constantly rekindle courage and inspiration for me.

Putting this brave philosophy into practice is easier said than done, but I am doing it, because I am one of Christ's living *"witnesses."* Ac.5:32 My life has purpose. I am part of a hurting world. God and His healing grace are reflected through me. I am vital to His Love-plan for people.

I have written this book to share some of the lessons I have learned since Daisy's demise, in the hope that others may discover, as I have, *how much there is to keep living for*.

If this book heals some pain and clarifies some answers; if it helps people to value life—*even when the scenery changes*, and if it motivates a fresh embrace of memories with a positive perspective, inducing a re-focus on God's miracle-Love, then it will be worth all the tears that I have shed while writing these pages.

WHY? TRAGEDY TRAUMA TRIUMPH

Prayer By T.L.

"Sustain Me, Lord!"

Lord, I reach to touch You,
There's so very much to do.
When bereavement overcomes me,
My strength must come from You.

I've released my darling Daisy;
She's with You there above.
She's always walked beside me,
My companion whom I love.

I feel so lost and lonely,
And, though I do believe,
I need You Lord, to hold me,
To help me not to grieve.

Please give me strength and courage,
Lord, to bear what I must bear,
When loneliness assails me,
I'll remember that You're there.

Fuel hope for my tomorrows,
I know Life must go on.
I'm believing that my darkness
Will be followed by the dawn.

You've led us throughout all the world,
From shore to distant shore.
Sustain me, Lord, 'til I'm through this
And I am strong once more.

T.L. Osborn — July 5, 1995

CHAPTER ONE

CHRONICLE FROM NOVOSIBIRSK, SIBERIA

I AM HERE in the third city of the ex-Soviet Union, *Novosibirsk*. This is the cultural and economic capital of the vast Siberian region. I am alone in my small hotel room. It measures 7½ by 12 feet in size and there is a 4½ by 6 foot space for a toilet stool, a basin and a tiny tub—with only cold water. I have a few hours before our plane leaves, so I decided to begin this chronicle.

THE NIGHT OF NIGHTS

It was just over a year ago that I experienced the most traumatic event of my life. My darling wife and teammate, Daisy Marie, was breathing her last, transcending earthly mortality, penetrating the veil that separates us from the invisible world, to be forever with her Lord.

Daughter LaDonna and granddaughters, Daneesa and LaVona, had been with us for two nights. (Our dear friend and assistant, Karen Anaya, had been with Daisy and me on a round-the-clock vigil.)

The Final Hours

A special acquaintance of ours, the head-nurse at the Oral Roberts hospital, had heard Daisy preach at the Mabee Center. Being aware of our crisis, she came to our house directly from the hospital, after a full day on duty, to be of assistance to us. She stayed all night then returned to her management post, without sleep. After another day on hospital duty—and still without rest, she came again from work to be with us. As a medical professional, she was aware, more than we, of what was taking place.

At 2:53 a.m. on the morning of May 27, 1995, my darling Daisy breathed her last as I was leaning over her, half-kneeling, holding her, gazing into her face that had beamed such responsive smiles and had brought me such happiness for nearly fifty-four years. Her beautiful spirit slipped away to be forever with HIM whom she had served so faithfully.

We Had Been One Now I Was A Half-Person

It felt like a big part of me died with her. I was stunned by terrifying bewilderment, slashed apart emotionally. How could I go on living with the best of me severed. It was a shocking amputation of all that was vital to me.

We had met and married when we were very young. We had practically raised each other. We loved each other. We were *one.* How could I survive as a *half*-person? I felt I was being siphoned into a vacuum of terrifying emptiness.

Daisy's body was not breathing—it was motionless. This beautiful, dynamic person who had brightened my life for nearly fifty-four years had slipped beyond my reach. She was no more. I held her inert body in my grasp. I could not let her go. She had been my life, my joy, my world. Flashbacks of our beginnings appeared across the screen of my mind.

The Girl I met At Almo

I saw the sixteen-year-old girl who came into the little church at Almo, California, where Rev. Ernest Dillard and I were conducting a revival meeting. Back in Oklahoma, my father had permitted me to go with him when I was only sixteen, to play music in the revival meetings. A friend had invited us to conduct a series of special meetings in his little church at Almo.

Twenty miles to the west was Los Banos. Daisy lived on a farm near there. She and some church friends had heard about the Oklahoma revivalists at Almo and had come to visit the meetings.

I had spotted her when she entered the building; blond, beautiful, serene, energetic, smart.

T.L. met Daisy in Almo, California where she came with friends from Los Banos to attend a revival meeting conducted by Oklahoma Evangelists Ernest Dillard and his young musical helper, Tommy Osborn. Their courtship had to be by mail, and they were married one year later.

And she had been impressed by my music, testimony, and commitment in gospel ministry.

I knew that I must meet this unique and remarkable young believer. An older gentleman introduced us. Everything in me became vibrant with life when I looked into her eyes and we shook hands. *This* was the lady—no doubt about it—with whom I yearned to share my life.

I Proposed To Daisy

Due to our revival schedule, and having no money of my own, Daisy and I managed, with great difficulty, to get to see each other only three or four times before Rev. Dillard decided to return to Oklahoma.

During our last brief visit at a church in Turlock, I proposed to her. I realized that my proposition was abrupt but I had no alternative. We were leaving the state. Thank God, Daisy accepted my impulsive proposal, believing in my commitment to her. She risked letting herself fall in love with this itinerant young preacher despite the ridicule and negative predictions of high school peers.

Courtship By Correspondence

Our courtship had to be by correspondence. I had no money for telephone calls so we wrote letters. One year later, we were married in the little

Full Gospel Church at Los Banos. I had borrowed a suit from my brother-in-law, and had budgeted my precious few dollars to include a white carnation corsage for Daisy and a boutonniere for me. To make ends meet, I managed a ride from Oklahoma to California with a couple who was driving west. But my ride stopped a hundred miles short of Los Banos, so I had to hitchhike the final lap of my journey.

The day after our wedding, we began our trip back to Sand Springs, Oklahoma, where I had a job. We arrived with fifty-two cents. I had measured my few dollars very carefully.

I was burning to get back into the ministry of evangelism. I traded my only possessions, a cow and a calf at my father's farm, for a 1930 Model A Ford coupe. With twenty dollars from my brother, Lonnie, we overhauled the engine, and with thirty-five dollars from Daisy's brother, Bud, we made it back to California. Then we sold the car for needed cash and began our preaching career in a church at Campbell, California, whose pastor had invited us to conduct a revival.

After that and other such meetings in California, we went to Portland, Oregon to establish a new church. From there, we went to India as missionaries, but returned without success. After ten months we were back in Portland where we learned about the miraculous. With our new knowledge about miracles, and with fresh faith, we went abroad again — this time with great success. That success was repeated in seventy-three nations during more than a half-century of mass miracle evangelism that has affected foreign missions and gospel evangelism policy worldwide.

HER UNRELENTING OPTIMISM

None of that would have happened without the inspiration and dynamic encouragement of wonderful Daisy, the gallant woman of God who had been my wife. In our nearly fifty-four years together, we had never had an argument. I never heard her speak or hint a negative word or thought. Never had I seen her hesitate in life-threatening circumstances.

This vivacious lady had cheered me, encouraged me, believed with me in ministry, and had been a source of constant and unrelenting optimism, solace and reassuring buoyancy. She was indomitable in spirit, relentless in courage, dynamic in attitude, positive in planning, incredibly generous in giving, powerful in witness and ministry, inspiring in life, dedicated in service to people, determined in crusades, faithful in love.

Now, I was holding in my arms the physical remains of this beloved teammate. Her spirit was gone. Her mortal house of clay was empty. Her life had been fulfilled. She was motionless. I could not comprehend life without Daisy's exhilarating companionship.

All I had ever accomplished in ministry had sprung from her reassuring positivism and vivacious dynamism.

The Thunderous Question—WHY?

I knew I had to release her. She was not breathing. Her form was without life. She had always been so energetic, radiant with smiles, responsive, delightful, vigorous. Now her lips were static. They would smile no more. Her eyes would never twinkle their love-response to me again. I was paralyzed in bewilderment.

Like the earth-shaking impact of thunder, my whole being reverberated with the howling clamor of "WHY? WHY? WHY?"

"NO! Not my beloved Daisy! NO! It's too soon in life. She is only seventy. NO! Please, oh God! NO! Not this angel of light, this messenger of love! NO! It can't be!"

But her clay temple was without life. She was gone. I held her form, but it was empty. It gave no response.

In my disconcerted agony, I grasped for answers. In my desperate quest for mental equilibrium I rationalized, "I cannot ask, WHY? Asking WHY? is not asking for an answer; it is asking for an argument. I can't do this. I must release back to God the dearest treasure I have ever known."

But in my effort to bring my thoughts into captivity, the thunderous reverberations kept impacting me, "WHY? WHY has Daisy been lifted from my side? What can I do? Where can I turn?"

I knew my survival depended on me taking personal charge of my emotions. Daisy's mortality was a reality. I had to face the facts.

Ultimate Coronation

Weeping, I uttered, *"Dear Lord Jesus, receive Daisy's spirit. She comes to you now. Thank you for nearly fifty-four beautiful years together. Now she can be forever at rest. Her labors are ended. Her mission is completed. No more toiling — no more tears. This is the ultimate coronation for her precious and radiant life."*

Oh the vacuum that I sensed knowing that she was no longer in that temple of clay that had housed her beautiful spirit for over seventy years and that had brought me such companionship and love. Her precious body was still!

Alone And Terrified

An emptiness engulfed me that I never knew existed. Something in me seemed to die with Daisy. What could I do? Where could I turn? What was life without my companion? She had meant everything to me. She was my joy, my love, my inspiration. I was seized by terrifying fright. I knew that I faced the greatest challenge of my life. It seemed to me that a big part of my life and hope died that night.

For the sake of our daughter, LaDonna, and our two remarkable granddaughters, LaVona and Daneesa, I struggled to regain my composure. I lingered with precious Daisy as long as I dared. I could feel the warmth of her tender body diminishing. Her beautiful clay form was there but her gallant spirit was gone. All was emptiness. The spirit that had counseled, encouraged and inspired me for more than a half-century had departed. I was left standing in a deep valley of emotional devastation—*alone*.

CHAPTER TWO

TRUSTING God's GoodNESS

My PUBLISHING THESE memoirs, including painful reflections of the trauma I have experienced, is an attempt to share some of the lessons I have observed through my wife's demise and the lonely aftermath that has followed.

I have tried to judiciously examine the chronicle of events and to record for others some of the emotional healings that have occurred in my darkest hours, which have expanded my soul and have enlarged my life.

Tragedy or trauma arrives in many different forms — death is only one of them. In my case, it has struck me in the loss of my lifetime sweetheart and companion of nearly fifty-four years. It has felt like a huge dam collapsed, allowing a brutal wall of pain to sweep me beyond control, annihilating everything beautiful, leaving me *alone* and stunned by the ravished landscape.

For others, grave misfortune may come in the loss of a business, a home, or a position. Calamity and distress may be due to a flood, a fire, a devastating storm, a riot, insurrection, military or police action — or public anarchy. Heartbreaking and traumatic events occur. They strike unannounced. They can be frightening. They are universal and painful.

We cannot avoid these tough times in life, but we can control our reaction to them. Too often, people blame God for allowing them to occur when, in reality, He had nothing to do with it.

Blaming God Is No Solution

We may scream into the heavens, *"WHY God? WHY did you let this happen? WHY have you abandoned us? WHY must we suffer this loss? WHY do you not care?"* But these outcries of pain only exacerbate the agony. Bitterness and remorse never heal wounds nor solve dilemmas.

Because so many hurting people are suffering and sinking in this emotional quagmire, I entitled this book, *"WHY?"* I myself had felt grief so deep that I, too, was lost in the suffocating smog of ambiguous and enigmatic frustration.

Re-Focusing Memory To Transcend Tragedy

But I discovered a serene and biblical secret for triumphing over the devastation of despair and grief. I observed a new eye-opening perspective that re-focuses memory, transcends tragedy, and elucidates the value of *LIVING — even in an unfamiliar environment and with a re-written agenda.*

I want to share this new healing concept with whoever has been traumatized or wounded by loss of some kind. To do this, I have tried to analyze each tough stage of my odyssey through this dark valley of devastation.

Altered Landscape

Through sharing my loss and some of the lessons that have brought renewal and growth to my life, it is my hope that these pages will inspire strength in tough times, ease pain in periods of bereavement, seed courage to never quit, impel creative thinking strategy, motivate renewed resolve to rebound, stimulate fresh courage for new beginnings, re-focus the miracle of God's unfailing Love-power, and breed reassurance that *life is worth living — even when change has been imposed and the landscape has been altered.*

Faith That Triumphs
He Is A Good God

There is a faith in God that transcends these demoralizing events. Of this we can be certain, God is not the author of devastation and chaos. Humanity is God's offspring. We have an enemy whom the Bible calls Satan. He is the one who *"comes to steal, to kill, and to destroy."* *Jn.10:10*

GOD IS A GOOD GOD. He never sends evil, or calamity, or disaster. These are the works of the destroyer — the Brutal One.

God created Adam and Eve and then *"planted a garden eastward in Eden; and there he put those whom he had formed. And out of the ground He made to grow every tree that is pleasant to the sight, and good for food...and ...gold that is good, and bdellium and onyx stone," [rivers and treasures of all kinds.]* Gen.2:9-12 He created only goodness and beauty for humankind to enjoy.

Reading Ashes For Beauty

When Adam and Eve were separated from Him through disobedience, their lives became dominated by the Evil One — the Murderer — the Destroyer. The result: *"God saw that people's wickedness became great in the earth, and that every imagination of the thoughts of their hearts was only evil continually. And it repented the Lord that He had made them on the earth, and it grieved Him at His heart."* Gen.6:5-6

But even in the agony of God's anguish over humanity's disobedience and enslavement to Satan, He did not abandon them. He provided redemption through the gift of His Son who assumed our guilt and endured our judgment so that we might *LIVE*.

"God so loved the world, that He gave His only be-gotten Son, that whosoever believes in Him should not perish, but have everlasting life. For God sent not his Son into the world to condemn the world; but that the world through Him might be SAVED." Jn.3:16-17

Agony And Confusion

God does not send pestilence, disease, calamity and destruction. In the agony of confusion and loss, people look up and accuse God: *"WHY have you done this thing? WHY have you allowed this di-lemma, this tragedy to occur?"*

But He is not the Destroyer. He is the Healer, the Savior, the Provider, the *LIFE*-Giver. His will is never to send desolation and plague. He be-stows cure and recovery. He is not the author of disease and death. He *"forgives all iniquities; and heals all diseases."* Ps.103:3 God is the *LIFE*-Giver.

The GOODNESS Of God

It is *"the GOODNESS of God [that] leads people to repentance."* Ro.2:8 When tragedy comes, although we may not comprehend the reasons nor the implications, we can *TRUST HIM* for what His word tells us, and leave in His hands what we may not understand, being assured that *"the GOODNESS of God endureth continually."* Psa.52:1

I cannot understand why my beloved Daisy was lifted from my side, but I can *"abundantly ut-*

ter the memory of HIS GOODNESS, and I can sing of His righteousness." Ps.145:7

Proclaiming His Lovingkindness

Daisy and I have given over fifty-three years of our lives together proclaiming worldwide *"the lovingkindnesses of the Lord, and His praises, according to all that He has bestowed on us, and His great GOODNESS ...according to His mercies, and according to the multitude of His lovingkindnesses."* Is.6:7

We devoted all of our married life to being committed vessels of His GOODNESS, interpreters of His LOVE, carriers of his MESSAGE, associates with Him in His mission to give people *LIFE.*

Our proclamation of Christ has been *"a name of joy, a praise and an honour before...nations of the earth, which have heard all the good that He has done for them: and [millions have] feared and trembled for all the GOODNESS and all the prosperity that the Lord has procured unto them."* Je.33:9

Despite the traumatic loneliness of being separated from Daisy, my heart trumpets with the Bible prophet, Zechariah, *"How great is God's GOODNESS, and how great is His BEAUTY!"* Zec.9:17

No wonder David exclaimed four times: *"Oh that people would praise the Lord for His GOODNESS, and for His wonderful works to humankind!"* Ps.107:8,15,21,31

32

Even in my befuddled quandary, I can fully trust God's immeasurable GOODNESS *"knowing that all things work together for good to them that love Him, to them who are the called according to His purpose."* [Ro.8:28] (I am one of *"the called"* ones, involved in *"His purpose."*)

THE BiG PLUS SidE Of THE BALANCE

When the heart-wrenching "WHYS?" swell up inside me, rather than to question Daisy's *not being raised up* to continue with me in life, I ponder afresh, with jubilation, the tens of thousands of people who *have* been raised up in our ministries.

I look at the *plus* side of the balance that is loaded with multitudes of answered prayers, of triumphs, of victories, of healings, of miracles. The seemingly *negative* side of the balance that I view, with its baffling "WHYS?" because of Daisy's demise, can be surrendered with dignity and consolation to *HIS FAITHFULNESS*.

This one *seemingly* unanswered prayer cannot be justly weighed against the tens of thousands of *answered* prayers that Daisy and I have experienced. I can TRUST in God's *goodness*.

I am sure that even this one case of *apparent* unanswered prayer, though painful for me now, will eventually be shown to be on God's big *PLUS* side of the balance. I can rest in His faithfulness. He does not need to *explain to me the "WHYS?"*. I am consoled. I am satisfied. I am at rest in my spirit. My "WHYS?" have bowed in deep reverence to God's loving *GOODNESS*.

Yes there are tragedies; there are traumatic events in life. They may come in many forms. But through faith in Christ, *there is always TRIUMPH.*
2Co.2:14; Ro.8:31,37

The Victory Of Believing

In the face of my despair, I shout with the apostle Paul: *"O death, where is thy sting? O grave, where is thy victory? ...Thanks be to God, who gives me the victory through our Lord Jesus Christ. Therefore, [I can be] steadfast, unmoveable, abounding in the work of the Lord, forasmuch as I know that our labor has not been in vain."* 1Co.15:55-58

As I survey the unfamiliar vista of my lonely journey ahead, I am daily reminded that *"the earth is full of the GOODNESS of the Lord."* Ps.33:5 *"What time I am afraid, I TRUST in Him"* Ps.56:3 and He will never *"let me be put to confusion."* Ps.71:1 *"He [has been and] is my HOPE, [and] my TRUST from my youth."* Ps.71:1-5

"I will say of the Lord, He is my refuge and my fortress: my God; in Him will I TRUST." Ps.91:2 And that makes me like *"mount Zion, which cannot be removed, but which abides for ever"* Ps.125:1 [because] the GOODNESS of God endures continually. Ps.52:1

My Mission - God's Goodness

Despite my personal sorrow and painful sense of loss, life must continue because people need God's help and I, as any believer, am *"chosen"* as one of His communicators. My mission is to *"abundantly utter the memory of God's great GOODNESS, and to sing of His RIGHTEOUSNESS."* Ps.145:7 I am resolved that I *"shall be satisfied with God's GOODNESS"* Je.31:14 *[who has]* *"counted me worthy of this calling to fulfill all the good pleasure of His GOODNESS, and His work of faith with power:"* 2Th.1:11

As I continue my mission *without* Daisy, I am growing in awareness of His presence with me. My continual prayer is: *"Cause me to hear Thy lovingkindness in the morning; for in Thee do I TRUST: cause me to know the way wherein I should walk; for I lift up my soul unto Thee."* Ps.143:8 *"[You are] my fortress, and my deliverer; my God, my strength, in whom I will TRUST; my buckler, the horn of my salvation, and my high tower."* Ps.18:2 I have resolved to *"TRUST in the Lord...and lean not to my own understanding.* Pr.3:5

Even in my darkest hours, I have had the deep assurance and resolve to say as Job did, and without hesitation: *"Though He slay me, yet will I TRUST Him"* Job 13:15 because I know and am persuaded that *"none of them that TRUST in Him shall [ever] be desolate."* Ps.34:22

35

Light In The Valley

No, I am not desolate. *"Though I walk through the valley of the shadow of death [as I have done], I will fear no evil: for He is with me; His rod and His staff, they comfort me."* Ps.23:4 *"I have walked in mine integrity: I have TRUSTED in the Lord...I have walked in Thy truth...that I may publish with the voice of thanksgiving, and tell of all Thy wondrous works ...I will walk in mine integrity...My foot stands in an even place. In the [great] congregations [of the world], I will BLESS THE LORD."* Ps.26.

"The Lord is my light and my salvation...Though an host should encamp against me, my heart shall not fear...for in the time of trouble, He shall hide me in the secret of His tabernacle; He shall set me up upon a rock...I had fainted, unless I had believed to see the GOODNESS of the Lord in the land of the living...[and] He strengthened my heart." Ps.27.

Chapter Three

The Final Good-Bye

THAT HEARTRENDING night when Daisy departed from this life, the hearse was called and soon arrived at our side entrance. The couple in charge waited quietly. Their comportment was patient and gentle. They gave daughter, La-Donna, granddaughters, LaVona and Daneesa, and me time to linger with our darling wife, mother, and grandmother.

Frightening Finality

I finally composed myself enough to draw back from the bed in a sort of confused panic. Everything in me asked, "WHY, Daisy? WHY did you have to leave me? Everything of our world ministry was so dependent on your expertise."

Every day during Daisy's physical struggle, I had expected her to walk through the bedroom door with her arms raised, announcing, "Darling, I'm healed!" In my spirit, I saw that. She had always been miraculously healed whenever sickness had assailed us in our journeys. There had been numerous times overseas when we had experienced serious physical attacks. We always trusted our *Great Physician* who had promised:

"If you will diligently hearken to the voice of the Lord your God, and will do that which is right in His sight, and will give ear to His commandments, and keep all His statutes, He will put none of these diseases upon you, which He has put upon the Egyptians: for [He promises] I am the Lord who heals you." Ex.15:26

"You shall serve the Lord your God, and He will bless your bread, and your water; and will take sickness away from your midst." Ex.23:25

Jesus, Himself, relied on the scriptures as the foundation for His life and ministry of healing hurting people. We always rested our faith on the promises of God. He always confirmed His word as we trusted in Him.

Satan Tried To Kill Her In Togo

Daisy had almost died in Togo, West Africa. We never stayed in hotels because the cost was always high, and we could not assure that our food and water was clean. We always managed to get the use of a private house. There we could boil our water, prepare our own fruit and vegetables, and maintain some semblance of home-life.

At Lome, Togo, the little house we acquired was primitive. It had an outdoor kitchen and we drew our water with a rope and bucket from a well, then boiled it.

During our crusades, Daisy always went early, met with the pastors, and directed the meetings, then sat with the pastors while I preached, exposed to mosquitoes for the full evening.

A Deadly Form Of Malaria

We had always been bitten by mosquitoes in our outdoor crusades, but in Lome they carried a deadly form of the Malaria virus.

Daisy had, for the first and only time, been stricken by the disease and had become deathly sick and bedfast, unable to attend the meetings. It had been painful to leave her alone in the little house while we went off to minister to the multitude that had gathered.

Daisy's Triumph

Daisy was a believer. Although stricken, she never flinched. And God's presence visited her while we were at the crusade. When we returned, she was on her feet, dressed, totally healed and vibrant again.

She always received miracle healing anytime she was assailed. WHY NOT THIS TIME? Her beautiful form was now without life. We had been confident that she would rise up and be well. But this time, why had she slipped beyond our reach? We had never questioned but what she would be restored. We were confident.

Post-Java Crisis & Victory

Some years ago when we had returned from Asia, a deadly infection had invaded Daisy's throat and lungs. Her body burned with fever. She was bedfast and at times delirious, but she never wavered. One day I returned to the house from our office. Daisy was dressed, well, rejoicing, healed completely. We wept and gave thanks to God, as we had always done.

But this time, Daisy had not walked through the door with her hands raised, announcing, "Sweetheart, I am healed! Jesus has made me whole! I'm OK now!" To my dismay and confusion, she had slowly weakened and had slipped beyond this life, through the veil of mortality, into the presence of our Lord.

Why This Loss?

Memories of victories raced through my mind as I pulled back from holding her precious form. It was empty now. I had to face reality.

Daisy's body required certain preparation. Daughter, LaDonna, and her daughters, LaVona and Daneesa, would do what was needed.

Then the couple from the hearse came in and gently transferred her frail little physique from our bed onto the gurney, covering all but her face which they perceptively left in view for us.

INSEPARABLE PARTNERS—NOW SEVERED

Then they rolled Daisy's body from the bedroom to the outside door. We had exited that door together so many times, with plates of fruit or salads to eat in the refreshing outdoors, or with our Bibles to read and pray together, or with letters from our partners to pray over, or with maps, paper and pencils to plan crusades or seminars.

This was our last exit together. Daisy's beautiful and vibrant spirit was gone. Our *oneness* was severed. Half of me was dead. I clung to her form but *she* was not there. It was a brutal amputation of *myself*—of what was dearest to me.

As we exited the house, the covering was gently drawn over Daisy's beautiful face because of drizzling rain. I stayed close to her body as we wheeled it to the garage driveway, then paused for my last moment to be near her. When I summoned the strength to draw back, they slid the gurney into the hearse, then sensitively closed the door.

The click of the door-lock reverberated in my ears like the loud clang of a prison. I was locked away from my darling's physical form. I was severed. The amputation was final. I was only half alive.

No More Camaraderie

She would never walk with me to board another airplane. We would never again walk across the tarmac of some foreign airport. She would never be there with me again to greet the precious national people, adding charm and grace and vibrancy to those receptions.

She would never again precede me to foreign nations, meeting the pastors, government officials, and the press, to carry forward the complex details of preparation for a national evangelism crusade.

Spiritually Sensitized

There was a special anointing upon her life. She had been divinely gifted. Those spiritual talents always became active as she arrived in a nation to begin the delicate course of crusade prep-work.

She would become spiritually sensitized to local and national strategies, processes, methods of operation, systems, programs, tactics, maneuvers, formulae, designs.

She had fifty-three years of experience in grappling with the intrigue and intricacy of diverse governments, nationalities, traditions, cultures, and religious postures.

I had seen her suddenly announce, while sitting at a table or working at a make-shift desk, "The literature is here. It just now cleared customs." Or, "Our permit is granted. The papers are signed." Or, "I know which terrain to apply for. God has shown me." Only by the power of the Holy Spirit in Daisy's life could she have had this knowledge and supernatural guidance. It was a part of her when she was on location abroad.

The Ambassadress In Action

In a certain city, Daisy was awakened early one morning with knowledge that a border official was obstructing the entrance of our truck-load of *Tools for Evangelism* that we would present to the national pastors and evangelists. She simply got dressed, went out and hired a taxi, and journeyed sixty miles over rough road to the border.

There were hundreds of huge transport vehicles awaiting inspection. Ours was being ignored. The border official knew that if he held it back, eventually he would be paid a good price for the release of its special cargo.

In the extreme heat and dust, Daisy searched from border-shack to border-shack and from lorry to lorry until she found the official in charge, faced him, introduced herself and proceeded to tell him exactly what to do. He responded like a subject would conform to a Queen's orders. The materiel entered the country, without duty or *baksheesh*, and our critical deadline was met.

The Deadly Plot Was Averted

At four o'clock a.m. in another nation, Daisy suddenly sat up in her bed at a traveler's shelter where she had found a room. She heard a voice speak: *"Depart from this place without delay."*

She was there for a conference with the national pastors. They had come from the jungle provinces to meet with *Mama Daisy*. Their communist government had instructed soldiers to find them and arrest them because they were to be eliminated.

They could avert arrest and continue to minister in jungle regions where they could be protected by the village people and by the forest density. But they had risked coming to the capital, secretly, believing that they would be safe with *Mama Daisy*.

When Daisy received this message, immediately she alerted her Christian guard to inform the main pastor and the preachers, telling them to return to the jungle without delay, that their lives were in danger, that she had been told in a night vision to leave the place.

Daisy dressed, and called for her national-preacher host. With suitcase in hand, they went out onto the dimly lighted market square, hired a decrepit old taxi and ordered the driver to take Daisy to the border.

The head of police had been notified that the national preachers were in town for some event, and had plotted a roundup at eight a.m. The fanatical communist government was determined to eliminate them. Word had been passed to the president's office that they were in town to meet with an American lady preacher.

But Daisy was safe, and the preachers escaped to continue their ministries in the jungle provinces. (A further note: That evil-minded president has since embraced Christ as his personal savior, and has urged me to come to his nation for a national seminar and gospel crusade, to be sponsored by his government.)

She Wrote Her Own Contract

The anointing upon Daisy's life amazed those who were near her. In a certain city, she had been trying to secure the use of a stadium terrain for a gospel crusade. Several attempts to locate the sports director and his board had failed.

The situation was delicate because three armed forces were fighting each other for control of the government. In such anarchy with constant danger, offices could not function normally. Anyone who moved about at night was usually shot on the spot. It was an unreasonable time to attempt a crusade there, yet we had been clearly impressed of the Lord to go at that time.

Daisy was in the city, preparing for the event. Our meetings would be conducted in the mornings and afternoons so the people could get back to their houses or villages before dusk. But she had not been able to find a suitable location.

Early one morning, she awoke with clear instructions. "Get up, put your money in a basket (local currency was so devalued that an armload of it represented only a few hundred dollars) and go now to the big stadium field outside the city. Take paper and pen. You will write your own contract. Move quickly."

Daisy called for her driver, took her basketful of money, went to the stadium, slipped through the big gate of the ten-foot wall encircling the field, walked across the vast terrain alone, spotted an odd little shed, and was impressed to go to it. The director and three members of the stadium board were there in a secret meeting because of the prevalent danger in the area.

Daisy entered the shack as though she owned the place. She greeted them, expressing her gratefulness that they had come so early to meet her. They were shocked but so impressed at her fearlessness that they listened. She simply told them what she wanted and convinced them that God was going to bless their nation. She laid out her proposal and made her offer.

At first the director objected—and of course, he had no contracts available. Daisy simple pulled out her tablet and told them that she would write the contract on the spot. Because they needed money, and she had the cash with her, they agreed on the details and Daisy wrote the contract. She formally signed it, showed the Director where to sign, then passed it to the board members to sign as witnesses. They all did exactly as she instructed them.

That crusade on that stadium field turned out to be one of the greatest triumphs of our fifty-three years of mass miracle evangelism in seventy three nations.*

I never ceased to marvel at Daisy's anointing and how the gifts of the Holy Spirit functioned in and through her on location overseas where the spiritual need of the people is always so urgent.

---

* The entire crusade was recorded and the twelve audio cassettes are available, entitled *"YOU ARE THERE."* It is considered the most remarkable and faith-building series of the Osborn Ministry. It includdes every message preached by T.L. or Daisy, and the miracles—as they took place and were reported from the platform.

The story of that historic crusade is also published in the 510 page pictorial, *"THE GOSPEL ACCORDING TO T.L. & DAISY"*—the saga of their apostolic ministry in 70 nations, including vivid visitations and explicit experiences. With 324 scripture references and 489 photos, it is an unprecedented chronicle of faith in action. Nothing else like it has been published. It should be placed in every family's home and in the offices or waiting rooms of every church, Bible School, doctor, dentist, lawyer, counselor, etc., as a living witness that *"Jesus Christ is the same yesterday, today and forever."* Heb.13:8.

The Dead Baby Was Restored

In another nation, Daisy was conducting a National Women's Conference in a big government Conference Hall. She had met the Head of State, then had addressed the entire government cabinet that had welcomed her, and then addressed the nation by national television.

At six o'clock one morning, Daisy was awakened and specifically told: *"Go to the Conference Hall now."* She hired a taxi and went to the hall. Strangely, the big entry door was ajar. Daisy walked into the arena, surveyed the empty auditorium, pondered what to do, then decided to go take her seat at the speaker's podium and wait for instructions.

After a few minutes, a bedraggled and frustrated woman entered the open door, clutching a ragged bundle in her arms, mumbling in anguish. Daisy stood to her feet and the poor woman saw her. She trudged toward the podium, muttering incoherently. She grasped at Daisy, babbling in her dialect, then thrust the tattered bundle into her arms. *It was her baby – and the child was dead.*

While the mother fell to the floor in anguish, Daisy embraced the lifeless baby against her breast, slowly pacing back and forth, wondering what to do, praying for guidance. Then, suddenly, from deep within her spirit, she commanded, *"O death, I adjure you, release this child. I command its spirit to come back into its body!"*

Daisy kept moving about, slowly, calmly, assuredly, holding the baby. All at once, she felt the little body quiver and she knew that its life had returned. She kept holding the child to her breast until its body became warm and soft, then she called to the mother, *"Mama, here is your baby. It's all right now. Jesus has restored its little life."*

She pulled back the dirty rags to uncover its face for the mama to see, and when she looked, she jumped back in shock, screaming. Daisy tried to calm her but she was awestricken. Finally she was able to tell Daisy that the baby had been born with only one eye. Now two beautiful eyes were looking up from those rags. The Holy Spirit, ministering through God's handmaiden, had not only restored the child to life but had performed a creative miracle.

Daisy was a gifted minister. I could recount innumerable incidents during which the Spirit of God moved in her life to bring about wondrous happenings for the good of needy people.

The Supreme Court Judge's Daughter Terminally Ill – In A Coma

Another example: Daisy was with a group of pastors in a certain city, looking at a potential venue for our crusade. A runner intruded with a desperate appeal. A Supreme Court Judge's daughter, who had been terminally ill at the hospital, had fallen into a deep coma and was thought to be dying. The preachers rebuffed the messenger; they were on important business with Dr. Daisy, and she could not be interrupted.

Daisy paused for a moment, pensive, prayerful, then quietly and authoritatively said, *"Take me to her."* They raced across town and led Daisy into the hospital room. She walked quietly to the bed, laid her hands on the lady, prayed silently, then lifted her voice with authority and said: *"Daughter, open your eyes. You are healed."*

The judge's daughter was restored that very hour, and attended the crusade with her father, to witness of Christ's miraculous healing.

Daisy Confronts The Witch Doctor

In a primitive nation, Daisy was again trying to locate a suitable crusade site. The pastors showed her various places. Then, passing by a certain area, they turned aside to visit the most reputed witch doctor in the region. He ruled the superstitious people there through their fear of large serpents which they worshipped, and with which he performed his pagan sorcery.

The witch doctor was intrigued by the visit of such a distinguished looking white woman. He came out to greet her with a large boa constrictor wrapped about his body. The preachers wanted to impress Daisy with the spiritual power and influence of this particular witch doctor in order to underscore the need for the miraculous demonstration of the gospel.

A Lesson For The Preachers
Witchcraft—No Match For The Holy Spirit

Daisy took advantage of the occasion to impress upon the preachers the fact that no power can withstand the presence and anointing of the Holy Spirit. She lectured them that, as leaders, they must understand that the power of the Lord is supreme; that they must teach that to their people in order for them to be converted from paganism and witchcraft to faith in Jesus Christ.

Suddenly Daisy had an inspiration to *prove* to those preachers that no witch doctor's magic could prevail in the presence of believers in the risen Christ.

She walked straight toward that witch doctor and commanded: *"Give me that snake."* He was shocked at her audacity; the preachers were dumfounded. He shoved the boa into Daisy's hands and when it touched her, the serpent stiffened like a rod in her hands. She held it as she admonished those preachers about the power of God and how His Holy Spirit was superior to any black magic or wizardry.

Daisy Did The Unthinkable

Then she did the unthinkable: She went from preacher to preacher ordering them to take that serpent in their hand and to hold it as *proof* that no voodooism could rule in the presence of a Spirit filled believer.

After those faint-hearted preachers had taken their turns, she took the constrictor and calmly handed it back to the witch doctor with a message to him about the love and power of Jesus Christ. As soon as the serpent touched the witch-doctor's hands, it immediately coiled back around his body.

This may seem extreme, but Daisy was a veteran in gospel ministry. She never did a thing like that before, or since, but it was a moment that called for *proof* that Jesus Christ is alive in His people, and that where witchcraft is rampant, the power of the Holy Spirit prevails.

Strategy For National Success

The national success of every gospel crusade we ever conducted has been due to Daisy's spiritual diplomacy, perceptivity, wisdom and expertise. She perceived from the beginning that for massive gospel crusades to affect nations, they must be planned with the knowledge and approval of the national government.

Whenever possible, Daisy would start by meeting the President of the nation. She felt that, as a foreign visitor, she should give him a thorough perspective of our purpose in coming to his nation. After that she would deal with other officials of government, pastoral associations, and the news media. Then she would begin the groundwork of inspiring the national Christians to become God's messengers of hope to their non-Christian populace, spreading news about the crusade to towns and villages throughout their nation.

But now, this valuable woman's expertise and leadership in world evangelism had ended. Her vibrant voice was stilled. Her wisdom was no longer available. Her spiritual stamina would no longer be felt by pastors and gospel ministers. She would no longer befriend and influence presidents, premiers, state and provincial officials to favor the gospel among their people.

I Felt The Anguish Of Millions

I stood there with the sound of the closing door of that hearse clanging in my ears. Its reverberations were mixed with the cries of a lost world begging for compassion, mercy, and understanding in leadership. Daisy was that kind of leader. I could hear the pleadings of millions in need of grace and gentle healing love. Daisy had ministered with that kind of dynamic tactfulness and sensitivity.

Now, her talented and wise leadership style was ended. WHY? WHY had she died? She had been so courageous, so committed, so willing to give her *everything* to help and lift and bless and save and heal millions of lives.

SHE HELD THE WORLD IN HER HEART SHE WAS A VOICE

Thunderous "WHYS?" blitzed me with their demoralizing and destructive suggestions. The world needed Daisy. Nations had been made better by her presence and capable ministry. She had held the world in her heart. She had looked at people with the compassion of Christ. Her tactful, yet dynamic strength, had lifted the needy to new levels of dignity.

The women of the world needed Daisy. She had told them: *"I am a voice announcing that your redemption is come, that your redeemer is here, that your emancipation has been declared, that your ransom is paid; and I am announcing it boldly to women and men of all colors, races, and nationalities."*

WHY had her intrepid and valiant spirit been lifted from this world that needed her so desperately? WHY had this love-messenger of *Good News* apparently *"finished her course"*?

As I stood there behind that black hearse, I felt the anguish of millions who have suffered loss, who live in confusion, who are stricken with grief due to calamity, hardship, misfortune, or tragedy, bedazzled and bewildered by the confusing on-slaught of WHYS?

Now I was one of those standing in that quick-sand of confusion. I had lost the dearest treasure of my life. Her little form of clay had been slid out of my sight, beyond my reach and touch, into the dark shell of that morbid hearse. She was alone. I was alone. The door had clanged shut between us. Our separation was final. Our union was slashed apart. We were still *One* but my best half was dead. What could I do? WHY had this ruth-less severance taken place?

When the door of that hearse closed, I felt the cold grip of death. I was dazed and stunned.

The Hearse Faded Into The Darkness Flashbacks Of Good-Byes

I stood at attention as the hearse pulled away from our drive and slowly moved into the dark-ness carrying my precious life-time partner. I would never touch her warm body again.

Alone in the dark, I stood almost transfixed, tears streaming down my face. I had stood in that same driveway so many times, with pride and pleasure, having helped Daisy into her car with books and papers that she would handle at the office. I had waved kisses to her as she had pulled away from our garage, and she had always signaled her love back to me as she had departed.

Daisy Would Not Return

But this was the last time I would ever watch her leave. She would never return to me again in this world. I was frightened, confused, disconcerted. My hope and my life seemed to dissipate as that black hearse, carrying my beloved, faded into the night.

How could I reenter the house. I tried to regain my comportment. I stood motionless, pondering the trees, the flowers, the bushes that Daisy and I had planted and enjoyed together. The drizzle had stopped. There was the patio with the lovely white chairs where Daisy and I had sat, talked, read our Bibles and prayed together so many times. I looked at the patio table and chairs where we had so often shared breakfast and lunch. Now it was empty.

It took me a while before I could go back inside. I knew I must recompose myself. LaDonna, La-Vona, and Daneesa were there. They were suffering too. And the head-nurse needed to leave. I wanted to express my gratitude to her. But I could not talk. My throat was closed tight with grief. Not a word would come out.

Chapter Four

Commemoration

GOD CHOOSES PEOPLE who are *"of honest report, full of the Holy Ghost and wisdom."* Ac.6:3 The Bible speaks of Stephen being *"full of faith and of the Holy Ghost...full of faith and power, [who] did great wonders and miracles among the people."* Ac.6:5,8

Following Stephen's martyrdom, *"devout men carried him to his burial, and made great lamentation over him."* Ac.8:2

In the case of Dr. Daisy Washburn Osborn, it can be recorded that *"devout women carried her to her burial, and made great rejoicing of her."* There were tears, but they were tears of gratefulness.

The Venue

The memorial service to commemorate Daisy's life and ministry was held in the beautiful auditorium of the building that Daisy and I had erected, decades ago, as the international headquarters of our global ministries.

Senior Pastor-Overseer, Rev. LaDonna Osborn officiated at the proceedings. The sanctuary was filled. Friends and gospel ministers had come from across the USA and the world.

Outpouring Of Love

Daisy's casket was positioned amidst a stunning embankment of flowers. Even the funeral personnel expressed that they had not seen such a copious landscape of floral splendor

A four-foot tall arrangement of white and red carnations, from Missionaries Bud and Fay Sickler of Mombasa, Kenya, was designed to represent the African continent,. Supported on an easel beside Daisy's casket, it depicted Africa's outpouring of love for her life and ministry.

Gorgeous arrangements, wreaths, plants, ornaments, bouquets, sprays, and all kinds of dazzling floral magnificence emblazoned the broad stage with their kaleidoscope of color and profuse fragrance.

They came from many national ministries such as the Roberts, the Hagins, the Copelands, the Osteens, the Schambachs, Freda Lindsay, the Crouches, the Hickeys, and from hundreds of other treasured friends in the USA and around the world.

Pastor LaDonna Officiates
At Her Mother's Memorial
(Partial script of the proceedings)

WE ARE HERE not only to *commemorate* the life of my beloved mother, Daisy Osborn, but to *celebrate* the homegoing of a saint of God.

And, we are here to be *comforted* — by memories, by songs, by expressions of love, by being together with treasured friends.

Also, we are here to *commission* those who have been recipients of the seeds of the gospel that Dr. Daisy has sown.

In addition, we are here to *consecrate* our lives as believers in a way that God will receive glory through our living. Dr. Daisy has gone before us. Our journey is not ended. Reflecting on her example today will motivate our recommitment to carry the gospel torch to those still in darkness.

Evelyn Roberts' Letter To T.L.

Our family has had a long and dear relationship with so many of our friends here today. When Oral and Evelyn Roberts received the news of mother's passing, Evelyn wrote my father a precious letter.

She said she had been reflecting on her deep friendship with Daisy and how their lives had been involved together. She said that the Lord ministered to her, whispering that Daisy was tired, that she would never quit, so now she has entered into rest from her labors in the ministry.

I was pondering the years, the plane trips, the corridors, the crusades, the journeys, the meetings, the problems, the solutions, the criticisms, the labors, the long nights, the recordings, the books, the cameras, and all that goes with a life of ministry. My precious mother deserves a rest!

I wept when I read Evelyn's words because I had been kneeling by mother's bedside during her last moments. I kept saying: "Rest—Oh just rest mama. You've worked so hard. You've taught us how to work. You've shown us the way. You've been patient and loving, strong and enduring. Now, mama, just rest. It's our turn to carry the torch, and we'll do it. Yes, mama, we'll do it."

The Strength of Friends

We honor you who have come for this celebration. There are so many important people from distant parts of the world. We feel strength from you and I thank you on behalf of my father and our family. You are dear and precious to us.

These banks of flowers represent only a fraction of those that have been received. Our homes are filled. The graveside is already adorned. Thank you. Every flower, each blossom, reflects this profuse outpouring of love.

The Speakers

Today, different ones will speak to us. Archbishop Silas Owiti from Kisumu, Kenya will be the first. He has made the long journey to honor his special friend, Dr. Daisy, with whom he has worked closely in many national crusades, serving as the Chairman of most of the Osborn Crusades in East Africa

Then Dr. Margaret Idahosa, wife of Archbishop Benson Idahosa of Nigeria, will speak on behalf of the women of the world whose lives have been impacted by Dr. Daisy's life and ministry.

Pastor John Osteen of the renowned *Lakewood Church* in Houston, Texas is here with his wife and teammate, Sister Dodie. He is among the very finest examples of leadership in the Church today, a truly apostolic pastor with a world vision and a passion for the millions of despairing people in our troubled world. Pastor Osteen will share with us.

Then my eldest son, Missionary Evangelist Tommy O'Dell will speak, representing the family, and himself, sharing his own tribute to his grandmother. He is her first grandson.

After Tommy's tribute, my eldest daughter, LaVona Thomas, will read a poem that she composed after her grandmother's demise.

And Pastor Charles Neiman of the *Abundant Life Faith Center* in El Paso, Texas, will read a statement by my father.

Now, Archbishop Silas Owiti from Kenya.

ARchbishop SilAs OwiTi

DR. DAISY Osborn has revolutionized my life and ministry. I have known T.L. and Daisy Osborn since 1955.

I flew to Tulsa to meet them. We had a loving discussion about how to reach my nation and continent for Christ. I asked them to bring the miracle gospel to my people and they accepted.

CRusAde Prep Work

Dr. Daisy arrived to begin the groundwork. She appointed me as Chairman. I never met a woman who worked so hard.

She preached almost every evening during weeks of pre-crusade meetings, touching all of the churches of the province. We wrote letters, applied for permits, visited Provincial and District Commissioners, city council members, the radio and TV media, and the press.

Sister Daisy Osborn conducted herself with amazing wisdom, dignity, integrity, love, humility. She was a total diplomat. I took her to the top leading people, including my beloved President—more than once—whose heart the Osborns won completely.

The People Expected Miracles

I am here today representing the people of my nation. Any time we ever advertised an Osborn Crusade, the people expected great life-changing and irrefutable miracles.

They knew that wheelchairs would go back empty; crutches, canes and braces would be tossed on the crusade field and alongside the roads, because of the preaching of this woman and T.L., and because of the power of God's healing love.

On the opening nights, 100,000 or more people could be present. There may be more souls in heaven *from Africa* than from any other part of the world, because of the Osborns' crusades.

They tell the people, "Jesus Christ died and rose again. We do not ask you to accept Him unless He does the things He did when He was here. When you witness that He does the same today, then you can receive Him in faith as your Savior. Will you do it? And the multitude always answered with a resounding 'YES!'"

MIRIAM GARE THE LEPER

Whether it was Dr. Daisy or Dr. T.L. doing the preaching, God always confirmed them. One night, I recall a woman, Miriam Gare, who secluded herself under a tree at the edge of the multitude to avoid being noticed because she was not only a leper, but she was paralyzed and had to crawl on the ground. Her feet and hands were mostly gone from the leprosy.

That night, the Osborns prayed only for the deaf to hear. But God's love could not be limited. He came to Miriam beneath that tree, and His great healing power made her whole.

The next morning people came shouting at my door, "Silas, Silas, come and see!" I rushed in my car to the Jubilee Marketplace. A big crowd surrounded this woman who was healed of leprosy and paralysis. She was walking in the street to show the people how she was healed. She had walked until she was exhausted.

I rushed into the mob and took Miriam in my arms to my car and drove away from the crowd. She was walking herself to death. Since her miracle, Sister Miriam Gare always attended our church and has been a great witness that Christ is unchanged today.

Thank You America

My American friends, I have said many times, I salute you because you have produced wonderful men and women to share the gospel with *all the world*.

Today, we commemorate this gallant woman, Dr. Daisy. Did you know that she has ministered to more people than any other woman in history? Thank you for sending her to Kenya. She and her husband have won the hearts of Africa.

Thousands of people throng their meetings. Can you imagine twenty thousand people, or more, giving their lives to the Lord in one meeting? I have witnessed that in my nation.

I Am A Living Witness

I have seen the miracles take place—the blind, the deaf, the dumb, and the lame have been made whole. No one can confuse me saying that Jesus no longer performs miracles.

I am a believer in miracles, not only because I have witnesses so many of them, but because I, myself, am a living, walking miracle.

I was in a terrible accident. My beloved wife was killed. I was paralyzed. God raised me up and you see me today. I am well by His power.

WHEN I WAS DYING ...

Forgive me for weeping. My Lord wept when He found His friend, Lazarus, dead. John 11:35 But my weeping today is tears of joy because I am thinking of a mission of love that Sister Daisy accomplished which saved my life.

When my wife was killed and I was left paralyzed, the news reached America. Dr. Daisy immediately flew to Kenya to attend the funeral of my wife who was her dear friend. (I could not be present because I was dying in the hospital.)

The day *mama* Daisy landed at the International Airport in Nairobi, after flying for over twenty hours, she did not check in at a hotel. She knew in her spirit that there was no time to lose. She was led to take a taxi and come straight to the hospital, with her suitcases, where I was.

I had just been rolled back from the operating room. When I regained consciousness and opened my eyes, my friends I tell you, I was looking straight into the eyes of *mama* Daisy Osborn. They were sparkling, anointed and full of compassion. I saw her and I cried like a baby. And she cried too.

Expressing Love

I was in terrible pain. Both legs were broken. My arms were broken three times. And I was paralyzed. But I was not crying because of these things. I was weeping because of the love this woman expressed by flying to the other side of the world to be by my side.

She came close and asked: "Silas, can you hear me?" I said, "Yes, mama." She said, "God sent me to you. He told me in America that if I did not come, you were going to die. There is something in your chest that's going to kill you."

In the accident I had been thrown far and had landed on my chest against a big stone, breaking my ribs and injuring my spine. It had been terribly painful to breathe. The doctors took X-rays but I was broken in so many places that they failed to see that my lungs were punctured. I knew I was dying but I was too weak to tell them.

She Touched The Spot

God spoke to Daisy in America and she heard His voice and came to me without delay. As she stood by my bed, she reached out her hand and laid it on the precise spot where the damage was unbearable—on the exact square inch.

Then she commanded the pain to disappear in the name of Jesus. God's power went through me. I witness to you here and now, that I was instantly healed and have had no pain in that area of my body since that blessed moment.

Let me share with you what kind of lady this is whose life we have come here to commemorate. At their Mombasa Crusade, Dr. Daisy was preaching to the multitude. I sat there marveling at the power and anointing of God that moved through this woman.

When she invited non-believers to accept Christ, literally thousands responded. She prayed and helped them to receive salvation. Then she told them that the One who forgave their sins would also heal their sick bodies.

Miracles Signs And Wonders As Daisy Preached The Word

Daisy stood there like an angel of light and prayed with faith for the healing of people in that multitude. I watched as the miracles took place

Cripples threw away crutches. I saw wheelchairs lifted up as a testimony that those who were sitting in them were walking. I saw people tossing aside braces, canes and sticks. Blind people received sight and the deaf heard. I tell you, we are paying tribute to a great woman of God who has finished her earthly course and has gone to receive a very great reward.

After that meeting in Mombasa, the power of God was so strong. We were walking to our car amidst people who were singing and rejoicing. We saw a woman moving on her buttocks, paralyzed, unable to walk.

HEALED IN THE STREET

Some believers asked her, "Why are you still scooting on your hips when many are walking? Why?" And they were so full of faith that they began to praise God with that woman. Then the power of God came upon her and, to the amazement of people in the street, she rose up and began to walk. I witnessed that miracle myself. Dr. Daisy had preached so powerfully that everyone was affected by the message—and the Lord Jesus was confirming His word.

Here before us lies this great woman, this servant of God, this Ambassador—a diplomat, a missionary, a pacesetter. If she was laid to rest in Africa, there would be one or two hundred thousand people to commemorate her life.

I say to you, Dr. Daisy Osborn, my dear and beloved friend, "May you rest in peace. Thank you for your life and example."

Dr. Margaret Idahosa

I STAND HERE today to salute *mom* Daisy because of what she means to the lives of men and women in my nation of Nigeria, and in the whole world.

This great woman is a General, a legend of our time, a fearless woman, full of love, dignity, and integrity. I met her some years back and she has never changed.

I am the wife of Archbishop Benson Idahosa. When I first knew *mom* Daisy, we were pastors of a small church. Women were to be subservient—seen and not heard—in the background, mainly producing babies.

Mama Daisy Found Me

When Dr. Daisy Osborn and Dr. T.L. came to my city for a great crusade, I usually sat at the back of our church because there was no place for me to minister, and even before the benediction, I was gone. Then this woman and her husband came.

A hundred thousand people came to hear them. It sounds unreal but it is true. During their crusade in our city, Dr. Daisy said to my husband, "Benson, where is your wife?" And he answered, "She's somewhere."

There were no seats at the crusade. The people stood and listened and believed and received their miracles. The meetings finished very late. Night after night, I would run home after the meetings closed.

I Was A Nobody
I Never Knew I Had Gifts

One night, after Dr. Daisy finished ministering at the crusade, she made the driver bring her to my house, determined to find me. She stood outside and called: "Where is Benson's wife?" I heard her and was afraid, but I came out and said, "Yes ma. This is me." Then she said, "I want to see you tomorrow." And she left.

My heart was pounding. Why was this woman determined to see me? The next morning I went to her hotel. She sat me down and talked for a long time. Her words and her love changed my life.

Dr. Daisy was my mentor. She found me when I was a nobody, and brought me all the way up to the pulpit and to world leadership among women.

I never knew that I had gifts and talents. I never knew that I could preach and that God would confirm me with miracles in the same way that He confirms my husband. I never knew that I was valuable or pretty. I never knew that I had something to offer my generation.

I Had A New Beginning

But it was this woman, Dr. Daisy, who sat and talked to me for more than two hours. Ever since, if I have a problem, if I'm disappointed, if I'm discouraged, all I need to is to call *Mama* Daisy.

We call her Mama Daisy. Her name is a household word in my country. Anywhere, even in the remotest villages, they know about Dr. Daisy and T.L.

Even though she is not with us today, the seeds that she has sown in Africa—and in my life—will live and keep on producing fruit forever. Daisy lives in me. She is not gone from me. She lives in my house. Her ministry continues through me—and through thousands of other women.

They Ordained Me For Ministry

Dr. Daisy and T.L. ordained me for the ministry when to do that was *taboo* in Africa. When I returned home, with my beautiful *Certificate of Ordination*, people—and some leaders—were shocked.

Very soon, my husband and I began ordaining women into the ministry. Now African women are building churches, pastoring, evangelizing, and doing everything that any gospel minister can do, in at least seventeen nations of our continent.

The Vision — Daisy's Encouragement

A few years ago, God gave me a vision for the women of Africa. I shared that vision with Mama Daisy. She said, "Margaret, go for it!"

We all met and she became our international advisor for the Christian Women's Fellowship International. We now have chapters in seventeen nations of Africa and in other nations around the world.

Today Mama Daisy is not with us, but her seed will live forever.

The Bible says, *"Tell your children and let your children tell their children, and their children the next generation."* Joel 1:3

We Will Tell Our Children

I say to you today, Mama Daisy—because I think you are hearing me—: The seed that you sowed in me and in the lives of women and men in Africa, will keep producing fruit. We will tell it to our children and our children will tell their children and their children will tell the next generation.

I salute you Mom. You meant so much to us—to me, to my husband, to our children. You are resting from your labor now. Rest in peace. We will carry on the message you taught us; we will run with the vision; we will publish it so that others will also run with it—until Jesus comes.

PASTOR JOHN OSTEEN
Lakewood Church - Houston, Texas

BROTHER SILAS OWITI and Sister Margaret Idahosa have spoken eloquently today. What more can I say? These two powerful leaders represent Africa. But many nations of the world could give similar tributes.

We thank God for every hour that Sister Daisy flew on those planes, every restless night she spent abroad, every moment she journeyed and toiled, with a tired body, as she gave of herself to reach suffering humanity for our Lord. Only God knows what she has accomplished for the peoples of our troubled world.

The Influence Of This Couple

As we reflect on the fruitful life of this gallant woman of God, I represent the many ministers and preachers who have been influenced and inspired by her life and example in sharing Christ with our world. Hundreds of thousands of preachers all around the globe have been enriched by the lives of this anointed woman and her husband.

When you talk about Daisy, you talk about T.L. When you talk about T.L. you talk about Daisy. They are inseparable—always have been. Only heaven will record how many ministers are preaching the gospel today because of them.

I feel so blessed to have known them both. When I first heard about the Osborns, I read their book, *"Healing the Sick and Casting Out Devils."* I said, "I must find this couple." I wept when I saw the pictures of the multitudes and of the miracles.

As a Baptist minister who had just received the baptism of the Holy Ghost, I had not believed that these things could happen in our day. I pondered: Are these miracles real? Have I been left out?

THEY LET ME INTO THEIR LIVES

I refused to quit until I got in touch with the Osborns. They let me into their lives. I was determined to do something for my generation but I didn't know how to go about it.

But this woman and this man took me under their wings and taught me how not to preach *about* Jesus but to preach *JESUS*.

Daisy and T.L. will have a part in all that we ever do at Lakewood Church to reach the nations of the world for Christ.

THE INVITATION – THE MIRACLES

They invited me to attend one of their crusades. They brought me to the platform to sit with them. They put their arms around me and let me look right into the faces of the people who had received miracles. I mean, they made me stand right there and see those miracles, one after another.

T.L. and Daisy saw the hunger in my heart and they were determined that I should behold the glory of the Lord *in action – right there before my eyes*. As I listened to their teaching, witnessed those miracles, and observed the simplicity of their ministry, I concluded, "This is scriptural. I can do this."

For the next eight years, I went all over the world, and God confirmed His word wherever I preached. Then He spoke to me to come back to Houston and build *Lakewood Church* as a great world outreach center—a base for reaching the nations with the message and love of Jesus.

Daisy's Great Favor For Me

Not long ago, Daisy did something very special for me. You may smile when I tell you what it was, but it was a kindness that I'll not forget.

I had been involved in *Lakewood Church* and responsibilities of pastoring. I had not been overseas to conduct a crusade for a long time. I had done it during those eight years, but then when God led me to build *Lakewood Church* as an *"Oasis of Love in a Troubled World,"* I stayed in the USA and gave myself to pastoral ministry, with the exception of occasional missionary trips abroad.

Crusade And Leaders' Seminar New Delhi, India

We had decided to conduct a great gospel campaign and leaders' seminar at New Delhi, India, the capital of that enormous and historic nation. I was getting ready to go.

I had talked to Brother T.L. about it. I hadn't preached a crusade overseas in years and I had actually become frightened, wondering if I was up to the task. That may sound foolish, but it is true. I told T.L., "I think I have forgotten how to do it."

We had registered 3,200 pastors and preachers from all over India plus thousands of other leaders, workers and students. Although it may be hard to believe, I felt panic. So I called Daisy. I said, "Daisy, I'm getting on the plane tomorrow and I'm afraid I've forgotten how to preach." I said, "Would you *FedEx* me T.L.'s messages that he preached in your Hyderabad, India, crusade?"

I said to her (with a smile inside, because she and T.L. know me so well): "I'm telling you, if you don't send me those tapes, I'm going to fail in that big crusade and seminar at New Delhi. I don't know what to do. You've got to help me."

If It Works For Osborns It Will Work For Osteens

Of course, Sister Daisy laughed and said, "Pastor John, you know how to preach." I said, "Sister Daisy, send me those tapes or I'm a *goner!*" She assured me, "You'll have them in the morning, Pastor."

And she Federal Expressed to me the full set of T.L.'s preaching tapes from their Hyderabad Crusade, sending them overnight to Houston. I received them before leaving and I listened to them all the way to India. *And what works for T.L. and Daisy works for John Osteen because it's the word of God!*

Daisy and T.L. have marked me and my precious wife, Dodie. But not just us. Thousands upon thousands of preachers have been blessed and uplifted by their godly influence.

Dodie and I are thankful that we can be part of this celebration. Daisy has been received into her heavenly home to be forever with her Lord. Our day has not come yet. We are not home yet.

Welcome Home!

These accolades that we express concerning Daisy are beautiful. But I'll tell you, when Daisy swept into heaven, millions whom she had helped bring to Jesus were there to meet her. What a glorious *"Welcome Home!"* it must have been. Glory be to God.

She said, like Paul, *"The time of my departure has come. I'm ready. I have fought a good fight and have finished my course, I have kept the faith."* [2Ti.4:6-7]

That's the main thing for all of us, to finish our course with unbending faith. When God is through with us, we can go home to be with Him. Paul added, *"There is laid up for me a crown of righteousness which the Lord the righteous judge shall give me at that day. And not to me only, but to all those who love His appearing."* 2Ti.4:8

I salute you, Daisy Osborn, for what you mean to me and Dodie — and to our troubled world. We honor you. We will miss you. But thank God, one day we will all be together again.

Tommy O'Dell's Salute
To His Grandmother

I USUALLY PRIDE myself in being able to use words. But all eloquence has fled. A great one has passed and she shall be grievously missed.

I knew this treasured woman of God. Our private pain is exposed today. Her kind shall not walk the earth again until the world has changed. I vow to continue in her footsteps.

By divine grace, I've been permitted to preach the gospel to millions of people. This favor has been accorded me because of my Lord's love, but I think, to a great degree, it has been because of the faith and influence of my dear grandmother.

She Made Me Feel BIG

I don't see her there in that floral embellished casket. She is with our Lord. Only her temple of clay is here. She inhabited a wonderful temple.

I'm not tall physically, and Grandma was little. But her presence was so strong that she made me feel tall. Wherever she went, *she was big*. You forgot how little of stature she was.

Let us, today, recommit ourselves to the mission my grandmother lived for, the evangelization of those who have been forgotten.

My grandparents have gone to the whole world and many nations are represented here today. If there was time, they would speak from Europe, Asia, India, the Carribean, Canada, England, Latin America, and other nations.

There are some here today whose lives are not right with God. But rethinking the fruitfulness of my grandma's life has caused you to reevaluate your own standing before God. Surrender to Him, today. In your own way, make your peace with God. He loves you. He is reaching out to you right now.

I Thought She Was An Angel Incarnate

There is no way that I can express to you what this woman of God has meant to me. As a young boy, I thought she was an angel incarnate—an angel of goodness. To me, her house was where angels lived. Her spirit gave light to my life. She was precious to me.

When I was a teenager I was deeply involved in drugs and nearly killed myself. I left home at the age of sixteen and never returned. I dropped out of school and never finished.

Her Quest Persisted – I Was Saved

But grandmother's spirit never ceased in its quest for me. She was there when my brain was burned out and there no hope for me—I was a zombie—and she fasted and interceded on my behalf, as my mother did, and never gave up. When I was left for dead, Jesus came to me and healed me.

My grandmother's legacy is incalculable. She believed that the redemption provided by Jesus at the cross was for women as well as for men—that all of God's children are equal before Him.

Grandma, I will help spread that message to our hurting world, that women and men alike are welcomed by the Father, that His anointing is for His daughters as well as for His sons, and that it is for the same purpose—to be *"His witnesses unto the uttermost part of the earth."* Ac.1:8

Tommy O'Dell's Salute

I HAVE WRITTEN these words to salute my grandmother's exceptional life and ministry.

Dear Grandma,

I love you.
You have always been an angel of goodness,
an angel of light.
You, in generosity and kindness
are my trusted touchstone.
Beyond the limitations of the squalid,
retarded streets of existence
is the paragon of yourself.

I remember the lost years of innocence
when you were to me as the goddess of benevolence,
the vision of the most blest.
Beyond my mortal cravings
you gave me the eternal craving.
You were the most spiritual being in my universe.
Your gentle voice penetrated the clouds
of the serpentine coils.

You know what I am.
And, in spite of what I am,

I shall always favor the feminine
because of you.
I am forever in your debt.
Because, in my ignorance,
you showed me the wonder of woman.

Why did you, loved by a gentle man,
feel sorrow — as Moses felt —
for his comrades in hateful and loathsome bondage?
Because you did suffer empathy,
others may breathe free!
You are not alone.

I will continue to serve
as your representative of equality in our world
throughout my years before I am slain.
There is no death to the everliving.

Rest, Grandma! We'll carry the torch!

A Tribute To Grandmother.
By Granddaughter LaVona Thomas

I AM THANKFUL that I could be by my grandmother's bedside—with my mother, sister, and grandfather—when she went to be with Jesus. I will never forget the peace that was in her face until her very last breath. After she passed away, I went home and wrote this poem in her honor. I will try to read it to you.

Daughters Of Our Lord

I want to write about you, grandma
But I don't know where to start.
The memories that you gave me
Are such treasures in my heart.

There's no way that I can ever say
All the things I cherish about you,
Your love, your courage, your faith in God,
Well — that just names a few.

I close my eyes, and there it is,
Your radiant smile I see.
Your life teaches me to be
The best that I can be.

You've marked the lives of millions
With redemption — Christ's command.
You taught that God loves women
Just the same as He loves man.

From the highest caste, to villagers;
You helped them understand.
That they have value — they're redeemed —
They are vital in God's plan.

They are gifted by the Father,
They are daughters of our Lord;
And hand-in-hand we all can share
God's love in one accord.

Now you're sitting there with Jesus
Which is where you ought to be.
But all the seeds you left on earth
Will keep setting people free.

Thank you Grandma!

T.L.'s TRibuTE To His WifE
ANd LifeTiME TEAMMATE IN MiNisTRy

READ By PAsToR CHARlEs NEiMAN
AbuNdANT LiviNq FAiTH CENTER, El PAso, TEXAs

I WANT TO say some things to honor the memory of my beloved wife, but I don't think I can do it myself. I have asked Pastor Neiman to read my words for me.

After seventy beautiful years of life—fifty-three of them shared with me—Daisy went to sleep in my arms. Hers was the most precious and saintly passing into the arms of Jesus. This is the coronation of all that the Christian life means. It is the glorious victory of life over death. Daisy has now preceded us to the final glory of the redeemed who die in the Lord.

A Life Well Lived

She started so young and made each day count for Christ. She was saved at the age of twelve. We were married when she was only seventeen. We were pastors when she was nineteen, and missionaries in India when she was only twenty.

God gave us four beautiful children. We were called upon to surrender three of them back to him, two as infants, then our son, Tommy, an evangelist and musician, who went to be with our Lord at the age of thirty-four.

Tragedies Turned To Triumphs

Four days after his promotion Daisy — sustaining deep grief — was packing suitcases to leave for ministry across France, and on to Africa where we witnessed enormous crusades.

When we had to surrender our first daughter, the next week, a pastor asked us to sing at the funeral of a baby. Though grief stricken by our own loss, Daisy decided that she could do it, and we did.

It happened again, here in Tulsa, when our last child was born, then lived only a few moments. Within two weeks, we left for the historic crusades in Cuba. Daisy bore her grief gallantly. One day she told me, "Honey, the Lord has whispered to me that we will find our own healing in continuing to help heal others."

Year after year, she left her home full of conveniences to toil with her hands in making our lives on the road as functional as possible. In little houses, apartments, or third rate hotel rooms—often in primitive and difficult circumstances—Daisy's love and faith were consistent.

My Consolation

I do not understand why she was lifted from my side. It is a consolation to commit it all into His loving hands, knowing that *all things work together for good to them that love God who are the called according to His purpose.* Rom.8:28

About four days before Daisy transcended this life she said, "Ask our friends not to hold me here any longer by their prayers. I have finished my earthly course. My seed will run with the message. Keep the television off. Turn off the telephones. I want the room quiet. I'm watching for my Jesus to come for me. He's coming very soon. I am at peace."

Daisy's Pre-Crusade Work

Today we celebrate the homecoming of a brave and heroic woman. She has preceded me in campaigns all over the world — always going ahead to prepare the way with the government, with the press, with the pastors, to arrange the publishing operations, and to secure crusade and seminar facilities.

At my arrival, there was always a citywide reception to honor me. I cannot help but ponder the grand reception she will arrange with the angels for my arrival when it's my time to go.

Her Conferences Abroad

Daisy's Pan-African Women's Conference was attended by thousands of women. Today there are hundreds of those women in ministries, building, and pastoring churches, Bible Schools, evangelizing in villages and so forth. The same could be said about her great conferences in Kenya, Nigeria, Ghana, Latin America, Malaysia, India, and so many other nations.

Hundreds of women in India are in gospel ministry today since attending Daisy's Trans-India Women's Conference in Hyderabad. It was the largest Christian Women's event in India's history.

Recently, the same thing took place in the sports arena of Bogota, Colombia, seating 6,000 people. It was the largest Christian Women Believers' Conference in South American history.

We published over twelve tons of Daisy's five major books for the women there—in the Spanish language, and gave a full set to every woman who attended. We did the same in India and in other nations. Her life and ministry have affected millions of women worldwide.

In addition to her five major books, she wrote over thirty smaller ones. Her Bible courses, circulated around the world on both audio and video cassettes, are helping women believers to discover their *identity, dignity, equality,* and *destiny* in God's redemptive plan.

A Real Teammate

In our crusades, Daisy directed the meetings. She was the one who dealt with the governments, with the pastors, while carrying the full weight of our international offices and correspondence. In addition, she shared in the crusade and seminar preaching and teaching.

In nearly fifty-four years of life with her, facing every crisis and complex situation that one could imagine, I never heard a word or a comment or saw a gesture or a sign that was negative or hesitant. Daisy lived the faith, the hope, and the love, that she preached and taught.

Everything For Me Is Changed

As for me, for awhile I will struggle emotionally because so much for me and my ministry is now changed. I will try to rationalize what is self-pity and resist it, because life must go on.

With God's help, I will learn to live and to minister alone. There is so much to do and so many to share God's love and compassion with. I will trust in His faithfulness. He will not forsake me.

With God's help, I will carry to fruition the projects that Daisy and I planned together—projects that she did not get to finish with me. We have so much to share with the coming generation so they can benefit by what we have learned.

As I commit my darling teammate back to Him, I will draw great strength in knowing that you uphold me in prayer and with your love.

Thank you very much and may God bless you.

Daughter LaDonna Pays Tribute
To Her Mother

I HAVE UNDERTAKEN the emotional challenge of officiating at this commemoration of my beloved mother, because she lives on in me.

I will not let this occasion pass without lifting my voice in thanks for her life, her influence, her example, her faith, her love, her tenderness, her wisdom, and for all that her life represents.

But Mama Did!

They say that women cannot preach. But Mama did. They say that women cannot pastor. But Mama did. They say that women who are married cannot hear from God unless it comes through their husbands. But Mama did.

They say that woman's only role is to tend the house, love the husband, raise the children. Mama did all of that, excellently, the best — *and* she excelled in ministry around the world.

Mother loved family. Her mother was killed in a tragic train-car accident when she was only eight years old. She taught us the value of family. She has been the pivotal person in our lives.

My father and I, with my children and grand-children, will struggle with how to keep doing what mama did so well. She was a great wife, the best mother, an extraordinary grandmother, and a never failing great grandmother.

She Ministered Unaware Of Limitations

For many years, mother didn't say much about the limitations imposed upon women by church tradition. She just lived the Jesus-life and did what He told His followers to do, oblivious to what some said she could *not* do.

She lived and ministered almost unaware of the delimiting doctrines about women that prolif-erate in her own culture. She just did what God put in her heart to do, as a follower of Jesus Christ, as an anointed handmaiden, as a called out one with a destiny. *She just did it.*

The Female Part Of The Body Of Christ

But in the mid seventies, God began to show my mother the condition of the female part of the Body of Christ. Her heart began to beat with the women of the world whom she had seen op-pressed, demeaned and restrained.

She had observed how they were systemati-cally restrained and held in bondage; muzzled and restricted by religious shackles that paralyze the gifts God has invested in His royal daughters.

After ministering under a mighty anointing of the Holy Spirit—among the multitudes of the world—for more than thirty-five years, she heard the voice of God, and like the apostle Paul, she *"was not disobedient to the heavenly vision."* Ac.26:19 Christ appeared and commissioned her with the words: *"Daisy, preach the gospel to women."*

Benumbed By Tradition

God was raising up a woman—whose faith had been proven, who had known no limits—to be a voice to His daughters around the world.

Women are often benumbed by masculinized preaching and teaching and they can be lulled into comfort, leaning on their husband's arm, trusting personal problems and questions to male pastors, failing to discover the gifts and talents that God has invested in their lives.

The Power Of Good Seed

Daisy shook us up. She would not let us rest. I have to admit that it took me ten years to hear what she was saying.

But all the time, her powerful seed was getting into me—when I didn't even want it. Day after day and year after year, things were happening in my life that were causing me to become aware of where many women are in our culture. It's not easy for women. I began to understand that.

Yes, mama saw, through God's eyes, the world of hurting women for whom Christ died. He came so that He could set all captives free and extend redemption, with its new beginning, to all of humankind.

God wants men, women, boys and girls of all races, colors, languages, cultures, and of all economic, social and academic levels to know that He loves them, that He created them for His purpose, to be His temple, to be His voice, to be His reflection in this world, to give Him glory, to speak for Him in a hurting world. Every voice is needed. Every believer is called.

WE HAVE FOUND OUR VOICES

My mother stood in this very pulpit, and said, "Women we have found our voices. Let us never be silent again."

And I say, "We will not!" because there is a hurting world out there for whom the heart of God is beating—a heart of love, of commitment, of promise, of grace, of forgiveness, of invitation, of empowerment, of anointing, of vision, of identity, of purpose. And that heart beats in His daughters as well as in His sons—in all who claim Christ as Lord.

Every person for whom Christ died is valuable to Him, has a purpose in His plan, has a place in His kingdom. Therefore, we—all of us, women as well as men—will run with the good news. We will proclaim it. We will shout it. We will herald it. None of us will be silent. We have a message. We will announce the gospel of Jesus Christ to all people everywhere.

LORD, YOU CAN'T LEAVE US

I can imagine Jesus with His followers gathered about Him, as he foretold His departure. Mt.16:21; Mk.8:31; Lu.9:22; 24:6-7 The women were there with Him the same as the men. Lu.23:49,55

I can imagine His followers saying, "But Lord, you can't leave us. The world needs you. No one has ever spoken like you or opened the scriptures as you have, giving us light and life. The work isn't finished. Many religious shackles have not been removed. Walls of division still impose separation. Many are still captives. Don't leave us yet. You have just reached the place where the world will really listen to you."

And I hear the words of Jesus—I hear them loud and clear and firm. He said, *"It is expedient that I go away. For if I don't go, the comforter can't* come. *[I paraphrase.] But when the comforter comes, greater works than these shall you do because I go to my Father."* Jn.16:7; 14:12

In a similar way, we as disciples of Christ who have been inspired by the example of my dear mother, would weep and want to hold her with us because we know that the job is not finished.

Would We Go ... If...

Has it been expedient that she depart from us? If she did not leave us, would we go? Would it not be easier for us if she kept boarding the planes, walking the corridors, sustaining the time changes, trudging the miles, greeting the dignitaries, penetrating the markets, making miracles happen so that the gospel can come to people?

She did it so well. She knew how. She was an expert. Must we learn to do all of that? Had she not gone, would we learn—and would we *go*?

This woman whose temple lies before us today, has fulfilled her mission. Evidently, our Lord has said, *"Well done, daughter, you've done your part. You've been faithful. Come now and enter into the joy of your Lord."* Mt.25:21 Paraphrased

Our Time To "Be Fruitful And Multiply"

Now that she has departed, Yes! We will learn. We will go. We will carry the message. We will do the work. The seeds of her example and of her message have been sown in our lives. It is our turn now to *"be fruitful and multiply."* Gen.1:28

I challenge each woman and each man: Now we are the voice for this generation. Now we are God's representatives, His associates, His messengers into whose hands He has *committed* His message for all the world. 1Ti.1:11

Christ's disciples *continued* what He *began.* They had *seen* Him. They had *handled* Him. They had *heard* His words and had watched Him with their *eyes.* 1Jn.1:1-3 They were with Him when He gave His life on the cross. They saw Him when His body was wrapped and laid in a borrowed sepulchre. They saw Him after He was resurrected, and talked with Him for forty days during which He showed Himself alive among them. Ac.1:3

Today, you have heard His message. You have seen His life, His grace, and His power. You know that it is effective because *"it works effectually in you.* 1Th.2:13

THE NEXT GENERATION

After we leave this place today to return the precious body of mother back to the earth, we will take the seeds of truth that she has planted in our lives, by her example and teaching, and we will pass them on to our generation.

We will pass them on because it is the truth that is alive *in* us. It will continue to live and to procreate *through* us by the anointing and power of the Holy Spirit.

Be The Voice!

So I urge you today, "Be the Voice! Be the Voice!" You have read the quote on the front of the memorial program. Dr. Daisy said:

"I'm a voice announcing that your redemption is come, that your redeemer is here, that your emancipation has been declared, that your ransom is paid; and I am announcing it boldly to women and men of all races and colors."

That statement is what we are now all about. Not because of Dr. Daisy, but because of our Lord Jesus Christ, the redeemer, who has called us by name and has appointed us to be His ambassadors and ambassadresses to our world that is waiting for Christ's gospel. Hallelujah! Be that voice! Jn.15:16; Ac.1:8

Daisy's Victory Psalm

I want to read to you, as a tribute to my mother, parts of the 116th Psalm that was a special inspiration from God for her—she called it her victory Psalm. She wrote a date by it: September 30, 1990. That had to be right after the Women's Conference for Biblical Equality which she conducted here in this building.

I read this for you mother.

> ¹ *I love the Lord because He has heard my voice and my supplications.* ² *Because He has inclined His ear to me therefore, I will call on Him as long as I live.* ³ *The pains of death encompassed me...* ⁴ *Then I called on the name of the Lord....*
>
> ⁵ *Gracious is the Lord and righteousness. Our God is merciful.* ⁶ *...When I was brought low, He saved me....* ⁸ *You delivered my soul from death, my eyes from tears, and my feet from falling.* ⁹ *Now, I will walk with the Lord in the land of the living...*
>
> ¹⁵ *Precious in the sight of the Lord is the death of His saints.* ¹⁶ *Oh Lord, truly I am your servant, the daughter of your maidservant. You have loosed my bonds.*

The Bible says: *"By faith Abel offered a more excellent sacrifice than Cain, through which he obtained witness that he was righteous, God testifying of his gifts; and through it he being dead still speaks."* Heb.11:4 Daisy continues to speak in our world.

"Your Daughters Shall Prophesy"

The prophet, Joel, said, *"In the last days, saith the Lord, I will pour out my spirit upon all flesh: your sons and your daughters shall prophesy."* Ac.2:17

The Spirit of the Lord is on people today to prophesy, to speak forth the good things of God. We speak them with boldness. We speak them because we cannot be silent. God is raising up voices all over the world.

My mother lived her life well, in obedience to her Lord, faithful to the calling that she received from Him. The apostle John said, *"Blessed are the dead who die in the Lord...that they may rest from their labors; and their works do follow them."* Rev.14:13

We will follow you, mother. We'll follow you in death one day. But while we remain here, we will do the work—while you rest. Our hands are on the gospel plow and we will not look back. Lu.9:62 We will follow you and your example, as you have followed Christ. *Rest from your labors and be blessed!*

To The Family

To our family, I read these words by Paul:

"I would not have you ignorant concerning them which are asleep, that ye sorrow not, as others who have no hope. For if we believe that Jesus died and rose again, even so them also which sleep in Jesus will God bring with Him...and so shall we ever be with the Lord. Wherefore comfort one another with these words." 1Thes.4:13-14,17-18

Today, we look beyond this celebration to the day when we shall see our Lord face-to-face and be gathered with all who have gone before us to rejoice with them, honoring Him who *"wipes away all tears from our eyes,"* Rev.7:17; 21:4 *"and so shall we ever be with the Lord."* 1Thes.4:17 Amen!

DistiNGuishEd PAllbEARERS

WE WILL NOW be escorted to the Memorial Park for the committal of mother's body. Pastors John and Dodie Osteen will officiate.

One of mother's final requests was that her body be borne to its final resting place by women whose lives she has affected and who are ordained in gospel ministry. This guard of anointed handmaidens from various nations represents the new generation of seed carriers who will bear Christ's message to our world.

Rev. Chyanna Anthony, pastor here in Tulsa. *Rev. Marie Brown*, international evangelist. *Rev. Kim Francen*, international evangelist. *Rev. Deborah Ong*, pastor—Malaysia. *Rev. Christine Groves*, pastor—India. *Rev. Winnie Owiti*, pastor—Kisumu, Kenya. *Rev. Sergine Snanoudj*, pastor—France. *Rev. Donna Waller*, pastor—San Diego, California.

Commemoration Service for Dr. Daisy Washburn Osborn

Daughter, Pastor-Overseer LaDonna, officiates at her mother's funeral.

Ordained women from five nations carry Dr. Daisy's body to its final resting place, then stand guard during the commitment service conducted by Pastors John and Dodie Osteen of Lakewood Church, Houston, Texas.

Chapter Five

Reconciling With Reality

ONE OF THE first shocking realizations that I had to face occurred soon after Daisy's memorial service. I walked out on our west patio and sat down in one of the white chairs where Daisy and I had so often eaten our breakfasts. The birds welcomed us each morning with their songs. Fresh, beautiful roses opened to greet us with their radiant colors and fragrance, adorning our love times together.

Daisy Would Not Return

The realization broadsided me with emotional panic: Daisy would not come back again. She was not away conducting a conference. She had passed into immortality. She would never come out of that door again to join me on the patio for a meal, a snack, a time of Bible reading or prayer, a visit. She was gone.

The void in me was awful. My mind raced with thoughts of finality. She would never sit here again with me to read our partners' letters and prayer requests, and to pray over them with me. She would never hold my hands again as we agreed in prayer.

The beautiful person with whom I had shared my life, was gone. I was engulfed in a desolate void. I knew I had to reconcile with reality. As I wept, I surveyed the trees and the flowers that surrounded me. Their beauty was gone. Their reason for being had ceased to exist.

Bewailing The Facts Or Savoring The Memories

I knew that I must take charge of my thoughts. Yes it was true that Daisy was gone and that my earthly life *with her* had ended. God had given us nearly fifty-four years together. I reasoned that I must be grateful for those years and regain my emotional balance.

The most beautiful phase of my life had ended. Now I was facing life *alone.* I could face that fact or I could relinquish hope and abandon myself to despair. I realized that to question *why* Daisy had been lifted from my side would only aggravate the pain I was suffering.

I knew that Daisy and I had been, and I continued to be, among those *"who are the called accord-*

ing to His purpose." ^Ro.8:28^ God's perspective was greater than mine could be, so I knew that I must *"trust in the LORD with all of my heart; and lean not to my own understanding."* ^Prov.3:5^

LEARNING TO *TRUST*

My sister, Rev. Daisy Gillock, who was a pastor in Texas for nearly forty years, had been widowed. She and her husband had been teammates and sweethearts in ministry.

After Cecil's demise, Daisy Gillock was sitting in her chair, reading her Bible. She felt a tender hand placed on her left shoulder. She turned to her left to see who it was and saw sandals and a robe. Jesus had come to comfort her. He spoke these words: *"Daisy, remember, TRUST is the highest kind of faith."*

TRUST is having unshakable faith even when events or circumstances are not understood. Job said amidst calamities that he did not comprehend, *"...yet will I TRUST Him."* ^Job.13:15^ I have learned to *TRUST* the Lord on a level that I did not know before.

David said, *"The LORD is my rock, my fortress, and my deliverer; my God, my strength, in whom I will TRUST; my buckler, and the horn of my salvation, and my high tower."* ^Ps.18:2^ *"What time I am afraid, I will TRUST in Thee."* ^Ps.56:3^ *"I will abide in Thy tabernacle for ever: I will TRUST in the covert of Thy wings."* ^Ps.61:4^ *"It is good for me to draw near to*

God: I have put my TRUST in the Lord, that I may declare all of His works." Ps.73:28 The word "trust" appears one hundred and thirty-four times in the King James version of the English Bible.

HER COURSE IS ENDED MINE IS NOT YET FINISHED

When my Daisy passed from this life, I had to reconcile with new facts, new scenery, a new lifestyle. I was dashed by waves of panic, disorientation, frightening confusion. I realized that the only way I could survive was to face the reality of *change,* and to embrace this imposing transition, *TRUSTING* in my Lord.

I thought to myself: Daisy's earthly journey is ended. Her course is finished — *triumphantly.* Her coronation day has come. But *my* life is not over. I must not permit my future to be ravaged by this anguish of loneliness. This will not help to heal me, and it will not help anyone else.

A SERENE AND BIBLICAL SECRET

I discovered a serene and biblical secret for triumphing over the devastation of despair and grief — an eye-opening perspective. I could refocus my memory — *positively* instead of *remorsefully,* and manage, with God's help and grace, to transcend my trauma. This biblical secret would elucidate *the infinite value of continuing to LIVE.*

Instead of bewailing Daisy's absence as I pondered each scene of beauty and tranquility at our residence, I purposed to draw on my memory bank and *to place my sweetheart in each scene with me*. I could assuage my grief and draw comfort and consolation by *remembering our good times together*. Was that not better than *bewailing her absence?* Was it not more uplifting than the frightening void that was assailing me?

PONdERiNG THE POSiTiVE
RELEASiNG THE TRAUMA

I reasoned: Would it not be better to *remember* the beauty of our lifetime together? Should I look at those white patio chairs and weep because Daisy is *not* sitting there with me? Or at the yard and garden and flowers, and weep because Daisy is *no longer* there to enjoy them with me? Or at the sidewalk where we strolled together, and grieve because she would *never* walk with me there again? Or at the huge native boulders that we had brought from the woods, and bewail the fact that she would *never* sit with me on those boulders or kneel beside them with me in prayer again?

I placed photographs of Daisy, and of her and me *together*, in the rooms of our home. They stimulate beautiful memories for me. I was thankful that we had taken the time to record those photos. With cameras, we had preserved significant and golden moments in life together.

The chairs where Daisy and T.L. sat, talked, planned, read, and prayed together. Now Daisy's chair is empty. Rather than to lament her absence, T.L. has learned to treasure his memories of their beautiful years together.

T.L. and Daisy often knelt and prayed beside the big boulders they had brought from the woods into their garden.

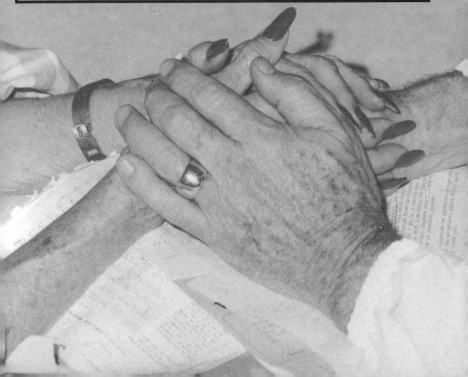

The Osborns believed the words of Jesus: *"If two of you shall agree on earth as touching any thing that they shall ask, it shall be done for them of my Father which is in heaven. Mat. 18:19*

Now that Dr. Daisy has been promoted to her reward, T.L. draws strength from his memories of the beautiful times he and Daisy shared as *"laborers together with God."*

Now I could relive those moments in my memory. Those photos have been a source of great comfort to me.

Glory And Virtue To Remember

Peter said, *"I will endeavor that, after my decease, you will have these things always in REMEM-BRANCE."* 2Pe.1:15 He was speaking of the *"grace"* and *"peace"* of God, of *"His divine power,"* of *"life"* and *"godliness,"* and of *"being partakers of the divine nature."* 2Pe.1:2-4

But in my case, the idea was to *remember* the blessings, the riches of life that Daisy and I had shared together, the *"glory and the virtue"* 2Pe.1:3 of so much that we had experienced.

Peter said in verse 12, *"I will put you always in remembrance of those things."* So I knew it was scriptural to REMEMBER what is good and pleasant.

Paul had said: *"Whatever things are true, or honest, or just, or pure, or lovely, or of good report; if there be any virtue, or any praise, THINK on these things."* Phi.4:8

Those treasured photos helped me to rethink and to reponder so much of our lives together that had been *true* and *honest* and *just* and *pure* and *lovely* and of *good report*—things that had *virtue* and merited *praise*.

I resolved to *"think on those things,"* as Paul advised. And I still do.

Peter remembered what was positive in his life. He recalled, *"We were eye witnesses of His majesty."* Daisy and I had been *eye witnesses* of so much of God's glory.

Daisy's resting place would be a monument of *"remembrance of His faithfulness"* in the same way that Sarah's and Rachel's buryingplaces had been.

THE POWER OF THOUGHTS THE MIRACLE OF MEMORY

To me, this was a profound secret for staying alive, for continuing to minister. I could draw consolation from my rich bank of memories.

Rather than to withdraw into the demoralizing seclusion of grief, there was another option. I could do as Peter had admonished; I could choose to *remember* the blessings of our lives together.

My memory bank was full of almost fifty-four incomparable years of pleasure, companionship, love, adventure, gratification, travel, ministry, miracles, messages, journeys — probably more far-reaching and rewarding than any couple who had ever walked together on this earth.

We had been sweethearts and teammates. Our lives were welded in a tender love and camaraderie that many couples have never known.

With Daisy's Guidance
I Repaired The Old Ford

When, as newlyweds, we had arrived in Oklahoma and had traded my cow and calf for an old Ford coupe that needed overhauling, Daisy had worked with me through the heat of the day, and had actually guided me in repairing the engine. I could work on a mule but I knew nothing about an automobile. Daisy had grown up with two nephews who were exceptional mechanics. She had learned from them about engine repairs.

She Said: "We Can Do It!
If It Breaks, We Can Fix It!"

She had always been an encourager. We wanted to go to California. We had no money. She convinced her bother to loan us thirty-five dollars so we could make the trip.

I was concerned that the old car might not perform. She said, *"If it stops, we'll find a way to fix it."* I knew that we would not have enough money to stay in motels. She said, *"We can sleep in the car."* And we did. (And we soon returned the money that we had borrowed, to her brother)

When the challenge was presented to us to establish a new church in Portland, Oregon, I didn't feel qualified. Daisy said, *"Honey, it's an opportunity. Let's do it. We can learn."* And we did.

"OTHERS HAVE DONE IT! LET'S GO!"

When a missionary from India visited our church and appealed to us to become missionaries, I was concerned about the risks that would be involved. Daisy said, *"Darling, other couples have done it. We will succeed. We'll learn the language. We'll work together. Let's go!"* And we went.

Our little son was stricken with cholera, but Daisy nursed him and he lived. For six weeks I lingered near death with typhoid fever. Daisy nursed me, day and night, and I survived.

NO MATCH FOR ANCIENT RELIGIONS

We had returned from India and had become pastors in Portland again. Daisy and I were both frustrated by our lack of success in India. We had been no match for the ancient religions of that historic nation.

We had fasted and prayed many days together, asking God to show us how we could convince non-Christian nations about the gospel of Jesus Christ.

We had become successful pastors in our organization. I had become the presbyter of a large district and the Secretary-Treasurer of our churches in four states. We pastored the headquarters church of our district, and were in process of hosting a very important conference.

Daisy's Logistics Were Right

During the same week that our conference convened, Gordon Lindsay had brought William Branham to Portland. It was said that God performed great miracles when this man prayed for the people. We yearned to attend those meetings and witness the miraculous, but I could not bring myself to abandon our conference.

Daisy reasoned: *"Darling, we went to India and were unable to convince them about Jesus Christ. We needed miracles. We came home but the WORLD is still in our hearts. We can always have conferences, but this is our opportunity to see MIRACLES. I think we must go."*

But noble man that I was, I remained with our conference while Daisy, with an eighty-five year old woman from our church, attended the Branham Healing Crusade.

That night, she told me all about the miracle meeting, sharing Rev. Branham's entire message and recounting each miracle she had witnessed. I wept. This was what we had longed for. I had opted for a conference that was not solving our dilemma. Daisy had opted for the solution to our lives and ministry.

The next day, encouraged by her example, I explained to our conference how we had gone to India and had failed, and how we felt that *miracles* were the answer to our dilemma. I asked to be excused from the conference and went *with* *Daisy* to the miracle meetings.

Thanks To Daisy's Initiative Our World Ministry Was Launched

That event, with what we learned and witnessed at the Branham meetings, proved to be the catalyst that changed our outlook and revolutionized our ministry.

We resigned our church and set out on our saga of mass miracle evangelism that took us into seventy-three nations during fifty-three years, and changed the traditional concepts of world missions and of world evangelism.

Millions of souls have been saved, many thousands of new churches have been raised up, and tens of thousands of national women and men alike, inspired by our examples and by our teaching, have become messengers of the miracle gospel in nations around the world.

That never would have happened without the positive influence and encouragement of Daisy. She had taken the lead.

With me or *without* me, she was determined to discover the secret of apostolic ministry. Her positive action motivated me and we made life-changing and world-changing discoveries.

Invitation To Jamaica

From our earliest ministry as healing evangelists, Daisy shared in the teaching and in praying for the sick. We had received an invitation to the island nation of Jamaica. We purposed to go, sold our furniture, mortgaged our car, and realized enough money for the journey and a crusade.

I did not want Daisy to go. I remembered our traumatic experiences in India. I felt that she and our two children should stay in the USA.

Daisy simply said, *"Honey, if you don't take us with you, you should stay at the airport in Jamaica because we will arrive on the next available plane."* Daisy never hesitated. She was always an encourager. We went to Jamaica *together.*

That was before we began to deal with enormous multitudes of people. We did what we saw others do. When the time came to minister to the sick, we instructed them to form long lines and we ministered to them, one at a time. Usually there were so many that the line was often divided and Daisy prayed for them at one side of the platform, and me at the other.

Miracles Signs And Wonders

We counted over a hundred and twenty-five deaf-mutes, more than ninety totally blind people, and hundreds of cripples who were healed during our thirteen weeks of ministry in Jamaica.

No one cared whether it was me or Daisy who prayed for them. The same miracles took place, depending on the needs of the people.

The Big Tent Crusades

Returning to the USA, we bought a large tent that seated five thousand people and conducted healing crusades across Maryland, Delaware, Pennsylvania, New York, Tennessee and Texas. In many of those miracle meetings, Daisy and I ministered to separate lines of sick people who wanted our prayers, and the Lord confirmed us equally.

The Amish Farmer
Cross-Eyed And Nearly Deaf

In Reading, Pennsylvania, hundreds of Amish people attended. They were shocked to see a woman who dared to minister with such authority and spiritual anointing.

One evening, an elderly Amish gentleman stood in the prayer line. He was extremely cross-eyed and was nearly deaf. He wore two old-fashioned ear phones—the kind that protruded from his ears like spools of black thread.

He found himself in Daisy's prayerline and was somewhat frustrated by having to face a *woman*. His religion had convinced him that women were not qualified to officiate in ministry.

Daisy received him courteously, asked him a few questions, then told him to remove his earphones. The eyes of the packed tent were riveted on her. She calmly prayed for God's compassion on this dear man.

Then she raised her voice somewhat and spoke with authority: *"You infirm spirits that have crossed this dear man's eyes and that have deafened his ears, I adjure you, in Jesus Christ's name, to leave him now."*

She paused a few moments, touched his face to alert him to look at her, and his eyes were perfectly straight. She spoke in a whisper and he repeated every word, then broke into tears.

Daisy was mighty in ministry around the world. Devils knew her like they knew Paul the apostle. *Ac.19:15* For over a half-century I had enjoyed life and ministry with her. But now, those wonderful events were only *memories.*

Reasons To Keep Living

Instead of drowning myself in the "WHYS?" of her demise, I knew that I must find ways to extricate myself from the anguish and pain of loneliness. Daisy was gone. My life and ministry *with her* were now history. We had been one flesh. Now we were cut apart, disunited. I could not pretend that it had not happened. We were still *one,* but half of the entity was dead. She would never be *touchable* again. Now, ours was a marriage between the deceased and the distressed. I had to discover reasons and courage *to continue in life and ministry*.

Option To Draw Positively From My Rich Memory Bank

Sitting on our patio that day after Daisy's memorial service, I made some discoveries—painful as they were at the time. I pondered the constructive option that was before me: I could draw *positively* from my memory bank, rather than to allow Daisy's absence to *dishearten* me.

It was my first experience of facing the continuation of life *without Daisy*. We had borne her precious body to the Memorial Park Cemetery in Tulsa. I had watched as she had been lowered into the ground there between the two beautiful pine trees that we had planted.

Sentimental Sentinels

It may sound sentimental to one who has not experienced this trauma of separation, but those evergreen trees gave me comfort. For me, they stood as proud and dignified sentinels, reaching out to salute Daisy's mortal remains day and night. Even in cold, harsh winter periods, they would be there and would always be *green*, representing our love that had never been seasonal, but always alive and constant.

I would visit Daisy's burial site often, but between visits or while I would be in other nations, those pines would stand there like faithful watchmen, guarding her precious physical remains. Somehow, I did not want her body to be left alone.

Those pines that we had planted seemed to represent a living presence there with her, and they marked the resting place of her delicate form that had been so dear to me.

Sarah—Rachel—Daisy

Daisy and I had emulated the example of Abraham and Sarah. They had *"bought a field for a possession of a buryingplace."* *Ge.50:13* Later, Abraham *"buried Sarah his wife"* *Ge.23:19* in the field which they had purchased. He himself *"was buried there [later,] with Sarah his wife."* *Ge.25:10* And still later, *"Isaac and Rebecca his wife were buried there."Ge.49:31*

Isaac's son, Jacob, felt strongly about where he would be buried. He told his son, Joseph, *"bury me not in Egypt;...carry me out and bury me in the buryingplace of my fathers."Gen.47:29-30* It was considered appropriate for heads of families to purchase a buryingplace. Daisy and I had done that.

Jacob was sentimental about Rachel's interment. She had died when they were in a journey from Bethel. He said, *"Rachel died...in the way,...and I buried her in Bethlehem"* *Ge.35:16-19; 48:7*

"*…and set a pillar upon her grave.*" Ge.35:20 Six hundred and thirty years later, her grave was still a monument to Jacob's and Rachel's walk with God 1Sa.10:2 as Daisy's and mine will be for future generations.

Enjoy The Memories
Or Drown In Despair

Reconciling with reality was a day by day, an hour by hour struggle. My memory bank became my comfort zone as I learned to replay the scenes of our lives and ministries together with *delight* rather than to drown myself in *despair*. Our years together had been good years, marvelous times, miraculous episodes, loving memories.

A poem by a bereaved person helped me:

> *I do not know what next may come*
> *Across my pilgrim way;*
> *I do not know tomorrow's road,*
> *Nor see beyond today.*
> *But this I know — my Savior knows*
> *The path I cannot see;*
> *And I can trust His wounded hand*
> *To guide and care for me.*

Dark Threads As Well As Gold And Silver Ones

The "WHY?" of Daisy's demise may always linger in some remote area of my mind, but it daily becomes a little bit easier to TRUST what I do *not* comprehend to HIM who *does* comprehend it all. Another bereaved person remarked: *"When the loom is silent and the shuttles cease to fly, then the Weaver may explain why the dark threads were as vital to the design as the gold and silver ones."*

I am learning to remember the beauty of life *with* Daisy rather than to lament the trauma of life *without* her. It is this choice-power that gives dignity to our humanity and enables us to transcend the grief of tragedy and loss.

Giving Thanks "IN" All Things

Peter said *"the trial of your faith, [is] much more precious than gold that perishes."* 1Pe.1:7 Paul admonished: *"In everything give thanks..."* 1Th.5:18 Not *"for"* everything, but *"in"* everything.

The words of the song express my heart:

> *Many things about tomorrow;*
> *I don't seem to understand,*
> *But I know who holds tomorrow,*
> *And I know He holds my hand.*

Each morning, I awaken with gratitude for all that God IS to me. I do not calculate my *loss;* I contemplate so much that *remains*—so much that makes me see that *life is truly worth living.*

The Value Of Choice-Power

Daisy's demise was, for me, a *tragedy,* and my loneliness, a *trauma.* But her homegoing was a *triumph.* Through my choice-power, I can transform my anguish and pain into a triumph for LIFE. The agony of loss is transcended by the much that remains. The pain of loneliness is transmuted by the memories of togetherness.

I have been blessed with more than a half-century of love, life, and ministry with Daisy. I am sustained by the knowledge and power of the gospel. All of that enables me to triumph over the devastation of despair and grief. Refocusing my memory has given me an eye-opening perspective that transcends my trauma and *elucidates for me the real value of LIFE.*

CHAPTER SIX

WITNESSES CHOSEN of God

I BEGAN WRITING this chronicle during the most difficult, yet extraordinary mission I had ever undertaken.

It was a mission to some of the major cities of the ex-Soviet Union: *Bishkek*, the capital of Khyrzykstan (at the foothills of the Tien Chan mountain range of west China), *Novosibirsk*, business capital of remote Siberia, *Perm*, principal trade center of the Urals, *Minsk*, capital of Belarus, *Murmansk*, the largest city north of the Arctic Circle, *Alma Ata*, capital of Kazhakstan (only 150 miles from western China), *Kharkov*, second city of the Ukraine, *Saint Petersburg* and *Moscow*, the ancient and the present capitals of Russia.

Daughter LaDonna had joined me to share in the teaching and preaching. Seventy years of communism in these great republics engendered spiritual despair in their peoples. We were privileged to bring new hope and self-value to thousands who had spent their lives under the God-less influence of Marxist-Leninist doctrine.

Healing For Russia—And For Us

LaDonna and I decided to minister *together* in these major centers and to *seed* the peoples of these five ex-Soviet Republics with the redemptive truths of the gospel. Jesus had said: *"The seed is the word of God."* Lu.8:11 And He reminded us that *"the field is the world."* Mt.13:38

I needed emotional healing for the painful loss of my beloved wife and for the loneliness I was suffering. LaDonna, who was close to her mother, had lost her best counselor and confidant.

We believed that healing would begin in us as we brought healing to others. We both knew that sharing God's Life with others would quicken His Life within us.

Daisy's Insurance Money

The check from Daisy's fifty thousand dollar life insurance policy had come. I signed it over to the printing company in Minsk, Belarus, headed by Gilbert Lindsay (eldest son of Gordon and Freda), to be applied to the translation and publication of Daisy's five major books in the Russian language—plus five of my books.

I wanted Daisy's insurance money to sow in the lives of tens of thousands of Russian women the truths that she had written, seeding them for dignity in God's royal family. If they could know redemptive truth and embrace it, they could become all that God had created them to be.

Daughters Discovering Dignity

God's royal daughters in many nations of the world were discovering new dignity and purpose in their lives through reading Daisy's compelling books. Now the women of Eurasia could be enlightened about their redemptive position.

Daisy's preaching and teaching had been powerful. *"The Lord worked with her, confirming His word with signs following."* Mk.16:20 Miracles and wonders always gave proof of her divine calling.

None of us dreamed that her preaching ministry would be ended so soon. But her recorded and written messages were circling the globe, bringing light, life, hope, and discovery to both women and men worldwide.

Truth – Spoken Or Written

Daisy and I had learned that *"the TRUTH is what sets people free."* Jn.8:32,36 Whether written or audible, its power is the same. The circulation of Daisy's books and videos abroad was proving that the same anointing that had rested upon her preaching and teaching ministry was being manifested in people's lives *as they viewed her videos or read her books.*

Paul, the apostle, wrote his revelation of redemption, and the Christian message has permeated the world as a result. The TRUTHS written by Paul have blessed millions with faith in God and freedom from guilt and condemnation.

Daisy wrote five powerful books. They would continue disseminating the *Truth that sets women free* – free from the limitations of antiquated restraints on the *female part* of the Body of Christ.

Why We Believe In Women In Ministry

Daisy and I had never sanctioned those traditional limitations upon women. I had been saved when a woman had preached. I had been pastored by a couple both of whom were preachers and who shared all pastoral duties with equal authority. When we returned from India, brokenhearted and bewildered by our lack of success on the mission field, it was a woman who preached the campmeeting message that lifted us from despair and seeded us with a reason to keep living and to continue in ministry.

My sister was supernaturally called to preach through a vision that appeared to her, as had happened to Paul the apostle. In a voice from heaven, she was commanded, *"Go forth and preach the gospel."* She established three beautiful churches in Texas.

Our daughter, LaDonna, had a vision of Jesus when we were in Concepcion, Chile. He made Himself known to her and later, specifically called her to *pastoral ministry.*

Include Women When Proclaiming The Gospel

Daisy had been given a vision in which she was shown the female part of the Body of Christ in its demeaned and limited form. Then she had looked toward a mountain at the top of which a blazing light shined.

Jesus appeared in that light and walked down the mountain, His hands signaling to her with the commission, *"Daisy, preach the gospel to women."* He specified *"to women,"* so that she would always INCLUDE WOMEN wherever she proclaimed Christ's message.

The commission to *"INCLUDE women"* in preaching the gospel was a profound alert to us that most gospel preaching is masculinized, addressing only males, generally ignoring females. We knew that the greatest psychological insult possible is to be *ignored.* We believed that the dignity of womanhood merited recognition.

Reediting Our Books
To Address Both Genders

Daisy's vision prompted a reexamination of our writing and speaking vocabularies, resulting in a reedit of all of our books to be sure that our language was *inclusive* – that it always addressed *both genders* – that it always "INCLUDED *women.*" Our books set a new standard among publications in the Evangelical and Charismatic worlds.

We were aware that the academic, scientific, medical, legal, political, and journalistic worlds had long since adopted *dual gender vocabulary*; that only the religious Fundamentalist and Pentecostal worlds were persisting in traditionally masculinized vocabulary.

Equality In Redemption

Daisy's lifestyle and ministry had been exemplary in many ways. It is a fact that she preached the gospel to more people than any other woman in history.

In addition to her administrative and crusade management expertise, she almost always shared the preaching and teaching ministry in our crusades and conferences. The audience never expressed a preference in who ministered – whether it was Daisy or me The same anointing was obvious to all and the same miracles occurred.

We had always believed that in redemption, *"there is neither Jew nor Greek, bond nor free, MALE nor FEMALE: that we are all ONE in Christ Jesus.* Gal.3:28 We had consistently shared all aspects of life, ministry, and business as equals.

Traditional Limitations
"Gentiles" Then — "Women" Today

Traditions limiting women in ministry today is similiar to the way *Gentiles* were limited in the Early Church. On the Day of Pentecost, Peter quoted the Hebrew prophet Joel and proclaimed, *"WHOSOEVER shall call upon the name of the Lord shall be saved."* Ac.2:21 He presumed that those words applied only to the Jews. *"WHOSOEVER — as long as they are JEWS — shall call on the Lord shall be saved."* It wasn't until the tenth chapter of the book of Acts that Peter and the Early Church began to comprehend that the prophet's words were *all inclusive.*

Wrong Presumptions

Today scores of scriptures concerning preaching and teaching the gospel are *presumed to apply only to MEN.* Tradition brainwashes people's minds today the same as it did in Bible days.

In the tenth chapter of Acts — over ten years after Peter had proclaimed those words of Joel — the early followers of Christ finally grasped the fact that the gospel was for *"whosoever"* of any race, tribe, nationality, color or gender. But it had required a divine visitation from God for them to understand that *Gentiles* could call on the Lord and be saved the same as Hebrews could.

It requires divine visitations from God today for women to perceive that *He* has placed no limits on them as His representatives—that only the hierarchical church has imposed restrictions.

Peter's Shocking Discovery: What He Had Preached Was True

Peter had a vision and was told to go to the house of a *Gentile*. Ac.10:19-23 He was so perturbed about it that he took a committee of Hebrews with him as witnesses. *v.23* When he entered the *Gentile's* *v.28* house, he spoke *"the Word of God…preaching peace by Jesus Christ: (He is Lord of ALL)."* *v.36* The power of the Holy Ghost fell on those *Gentiles* in the same manner that it had fallen on the *Jews* on the Day of Pentecost. *vs.44-47*

This was so startling that Peter reported the event, in detail, to his headquarters, and *"they held their peace and glorified God, saying, Then has God also to the GENTILES granted repentance unto LIFE."* Ac.11:18 At last, they had come to believe the words that Joel had prophesied and that Peter had so boldly proclaimed. Ac.2:21

THE SAME ANOINTING...
ON "GENTILES" THEN — ON "WOMEN" TODAY

Leaders in the Church today are amazed, as Peter and his committee had been, when the *same Holy Spirit that anoints and empowers MEN also anoints and empowers WOMEN*. It is time for "headquarters" today to be as honest as the leaders at Jerusalem were then, and to declare: *"Then hath God also to the [WOMEN] granted repentance unto LIFE"* Ac.11:18 and, as Peter said in his astonishment, *"Of a truth, I perceive that God is no respecter of persons: but [among ALL races and BOTH genders] whoever fears Him, and works righteousness, IS ACCEPTED WITH HIM..."* Ac.10:34-35

"WITNESSES CHOSEN OF GOD"
THEY WERE WOMEN

The record of this event continues with details of profound significance *for women* — details that have been almost ignored by the male clergy: *"They slew Jesus and hanged Him on a tree: whom God raised up...and shewed Him openly;...unto WITNESSES CHOSEN before of God."* Ac.10:39-41

Who were those *WITNESSES* to whom He showed Jesus openly? They were *women*.

"Now when Jesus was risen, He appeared FIRST to Mary Magdalene." Mk.16:9 Mary was A *WOMAN*. And other women were named. According to Matthew, Mark, Luke and John, these *women*

were the *first to witness that Christ was risen,* and were the ones who faithfully reported the news to the men. But the men *"believed not."* Mk.16:11

Later Jesus *"upbraided the [men] for their unbelief and hardness of heart, because they believed not [the WOMEN] WHO HAD SEEN HIM AFTER HE WAS RISEN."* Mk.16:14

The story continues about Peter's shock that *Gentiles* had been visited by God and had received the Holy Spirit the same as *Jews* had.

Women – "Chosen Witnesses" Commanded To "Preach" And To "Testify"

The record states that *"God raised up Jesus, showed Him alive – to witnesses chosen before of God [to WOMEN and later to men] and –* note this carefully *– [this resurrected Jesus] COMMANDED those chosen WITNESSES, [including WOMEN] to PREACH UNTO THE PEOPLE and to TESTIFY that...all the prophets give witness that ...WHOSOEVER BELIEVES in Him shall receive remission of sins."* Ac.10:39-43 Peter had received a revelation. He finally grasped the fact that redemption included EVERYONE.

Not only could *"whosoever"* call on the Lord and be saved, but the *women* as well as the men were to *"PREACH and TESTIFY"* that the gospel is for WHOSOEVER. Jesus had ministered to all races – to women and men alike. He had sent His followers *"into all the world"* to preach to *"every creature."* Mk.16:15 The Holy Spirit had fallen on women and men alike, and for the same purpose. Ac.1:8

THE TRAUMA OF TRADITION
THE TRIUMPH OF REVELATION

Daisy believed that we must continue to present the biblical truths about women in redemption; that women must be free to minister under the anointing and confirmation of the Holy Spirit. She believed that God will reveal the *equality of women and men in redemption* to leaders in the Church today as He revealed the *equality of Gentiles and Jews* to leaders in the Church then.

PRIMITIVE REGIMENTATION
ROMAN DEMAGOGUERY

There are only two short verses in the New Tesstament that advise women to stay in the background and not be heard or noticed. 1Co.14:34; 1Tim.2:12 In both cases, Paul was dealing with situations in which women were choice targets for arrest, torture and imprisonment under the Christian hating Emperor Nero, and cultures in which female pagan religious practices had to be confronted and restrained.

Women of *this* century are not living under Nero as their Emperor nor are they subject to antiquated laws, traditions and cultures that demean the status of womanhood—that enslave them as the legal *property* of their husbands.

In the modern, industrialized world, women of the Church are not converts from pagan religions that worship female goddesses, and should not be subjugated by the primitive regimentation imposed upon believers living under the demagoguery of the Roman Empire.

Local correctives by Paul for women of that primitive culture are not to be imposed as international mandates today, any more than *celibacy, footwashing,* or the practice of *slavery.*

Society has progressed. The Church has progressed too—in every viewpoint *except* her archaic restraints upon women in ministry. Daisy and I have never sanctioned those restraints because they are contradictory to the Pauline revelation of redemption.

ElepHANTiasis MiRACuloUsly HEAled

In Papua New Guinea, Daisy conducted the first great women's conference-crusade in that nation. Women and their husbands came from all parts of the country—by riverboat, by truck and public transport, on foot and astride horses and water buffaloes. Thousands of them gathered on an open field. The believers had agreed that the men would care for the children, on the outskirts of the crowd, so that the women could have priority of sitting space nearer the platform.

It was a pacesetting event. Those tribal women and their husbands learned that in redemption, there are no restrictions on the witness and ministry of God's royal daughters. Since those meetings, Papua New Guinean women have become involved in all levels of Christian ministry, establishing churches and Bible Schools, and ministering as evangelists and missionaries in unreached areas, sharing the knowledge of Christ in all regions of their nation.

One evening after Dr. Daisy had preached, she was ministering to the sick. During her mass prayer for healing, a man who had elephantiasis was miraculously healed. One of his legs had been like a watermelon. He had journeyed for three days to attend the meetings because he had been told that a woman of God was teaching and praying for the sick people.

His leg shrunk like a deflated balloon, leaving the skin wrinkled and sagging. Within two days, it had become normal. The men were astounded as they witnessed God's power manifested through *a woman*. It was evidence to them that women and men are equal in redemption. God always confirmed Daisy's preaching with remarkable miracles of healing.

God's Power As A Thunderbolt

One day she was preaching in the city of Kampala, Uganda. A woman had been carried there and laid on the ground. Her spine had been critically injured so that she could not walk. Surgeons had operated but she was left worse than before, and the poor woman lived with excruciating pain. She had begged friends to help her die. They heard of our crusade and brought her. She screamed with pain as they carried her.

While Dr. Daisy preached, the woman experienced a phenomenal miracle. The power of God struck her like a thunderbolt, and with such force that it bolted her onto her feet and literally blinded her (as happened to Saul of Tarsus when the Lord Jesus appeared to him.) *Ac.9:8-9*

She was startled by being struck by a thunderbolt with such force that it had blinded her, and was so terror-stricken that she had not noticed that her back had been healed. In panic she screamed for help, but those near her thought she was insane.

The Woman Is Not Crazy This Is A Miracle

Sitting on the platform while Daisy preached, I noticed the confusion in that sector of the multitude. An usher approached to explain that it was a crazy woman having a spell. Then a strange sensation came over me. The Lord whispered: *"That is not a crazy woman. That is a miracle."*

I slipped down the steps and pressed through the people toward the disturbing *brouhaha.*

The poor woman was screaming, *"Dr. Daisy! Dr. Daisy! Help me! I've been stuck by lightening. I'm blind!"* She was oblivious to the fact that she was up on her feet and that her back was well.

I took hold of her to calm her and told her who I was. She grabbed me begging, *"Take me to Dr. Daisy! I want Dr. Daisy!"*

I took my handkerchief and tried to remove the dirt and dead grass from her sweaty face and hair, than I led her through the crowd, up the steps, and interrupted Daisy's message.

I whispered to her, *"Honey, something awesome has happened. This woman has been healed. I think you might want to hear what she has to say."*

The lady grabbed Daisy and as soon as she did, another miracle took place. Her eyesight was restored the same as Saul's blindness had been healed when Ananias touched him.[Ac.9:17-18]

Then, that dear woman explained to the multitude how God had sent His power upon her like a bolt of lightning and how He had completely healed her back. It was a marvel that astounded the scores of thousands of people who were there.

The Victim Of Bandit Soldiers Humiliated Into Madness

Another day as Dr. Daisy preached, the sound of an angry, barking dog could be heard from the far edge of the multitude. Disturbances often occur during open mass meetings, so Daisy continued her message.

We discovered later that the barking was coming from a mad woman who had been kidnapped from a Catholic novice school by bandit soldiers. They had dragged her into their jungle camp where they kept her tied with ropes, raping her at will, day after day.

After weeks of brutal humiliation, the woman lost her mind and became like a mad dog, biting and barking at anything that came near.

Hearing about our crusade, some villagers had tied the mad woman's arms and feet, and had brought her to the meetings. She barked all the time that Dr. Daisy preached.

But when the time came for prayer, the power of the Holy Spirit came upon that poor bedraggled human creature and the evil spirits departed from her. She was restored to her right mind and was brought to the platform to testify.

In tears of gratitude, she held Daisy with one arm as she poured out her words of witness to the multitude. She pleaded for people to love and to forgive one another for whatever wrong they may have experienced. (The nation had been in civil war for thirteen years.)

It was a deeply moving experience to witness the miracle of God's grace and love in that precious life.

I had witnessed so many marvels of God's miraculous confirmation when Daisy preached and ministered to people. Anytime we were in ministry together overseas, she lived under a constant cloud of anointing.

The Moslem Intruder

One evening while I was preaching in a Moslem nation, Daisy was suddenly impressed to get up from her seat and go to the platform steps. She knew an enemy was plotting action.

She stood at the bottom step surveying the press of people. Suddenly a Moslem *hadji* wearing a *fez* bullied his way through the people toward the steps. Daisy had been alerted. She was ready.

As the man approached the steps, Daisy stopped him and asked what he wanted.

He responded, "That man must be stopped. He is lying. I demand to speak the truth so our people will not be deceived."

Daisy tried to reason with him, explaining that Mr. Osborn could not be interrupted like that.

But the man insisted. Finally, to calm him, she did her best to reason with him.

Daisy Challenges The Hadji

"Sir, I'll interrupt my husband on one condition. You and I will go to the microphone. We will call for someone who is blind to come forward.

"Then you will pray for the healing of the blind person, in the name of Mohammed. If the person is healed, we will know that Mohammed's name is honored by God and that we should believe in his message. But if the blind person is not healed, then I will pray—not my husband—but *I, a woman,* will pray to God in the name of Jesus Christ who is risen from the dead. If the person is healed, then you will know that Jesus Christ is the Savior whom God has sent, and you and your people will know to put your trust in Him."

The Moslem *hadji* turned in a rage, blustering through the pressed multitude, indignant at the words that this foreign women had spoken to him. Daisy was that kind of woman. Alert. Sensitive. Courageous. Compassionate. Attuned to the needs of people. A true *Ambassadress* of Jesus Christ.

The Bible speaks of *"Abel's righteous witness,"* and how that *"God testified of his gifts,"* by which *"HE BEING DEAD YET SPEAKS."* Heb.11:4

We all leave our legacy of influence after our earthly life has ended. Daisy has left hers, and it is rich. She continues to speak to us through her example, her books and her recordings.

Our *thoughts*, our *words* and our *actions* become the seeds of our lives that we sow — *our* legacy.

Daisy was an encourager, an uplifter, a fountain of wisdom, a patient and determined pacesetter in life and ministry. She was creative and always dynamic, never succumbing to skepticism, indecision, inconsistency, disappointment, impatience, dissension, or vacillation.

Although I cannot explain WHY she was lifted from this world of action, I take great comfort in knowing that, like Abel in the Bible, *Daisy, being dead, yet speaks* — as we all will keep doing after our days are ended.

Today Is Ours

We *do* leave our mark on those who follow us. We are chiseling the image of life that we believe in. We may not have tomorrow to improve that image, and yesterday has already gone.

But *TODAY is ours* and with our right of choice, we can improve our legacy to others. It can be better as we continue learning. That gives me courage to face each new day with purpose and gladness for the wonder of *LIFE*.

Dr. Daisy Osborn preceded her husband in most of their national evangelism crusades. She met government officials, pastors, the media, chose and contracted crusade venues, supervised publicity, and organized publication projects. Always positive and courageous, she was a vivacious gospel *Diplomate International*, known as *The First Lady of Evangelism*.

CHAPTER SEVEN

WOMAN OF COURAGE

JUST A FEW WEEKS before Daisy's demise, we had been busy working out plans for our next seminars and crusades in South America, Africa, India and the Far East. Also the events that we had scheduled in Colombia were drawing near.

TRAUMA IN MALAYSIA

During our mission to Malaysia, Daisy had fallen down a flight of marble steps and had fractured her leg. She was hospitalized at Kuala Lumpur where the doctor did not observe that the femur was broken. She remained hospitalized there for two weeks, assured by the attending physician that the leg would mend.

Missionary Evangelist Marie Brown, a cherished friend of Daisy's, had attended the Malaysian Conference, so she stayed with her at the hospital while I preached in Daisy's place, plus the sessions that had been programmed for me.

Following the conference, we were scheduled to minister together in a British campmeeting. I had to do one of the most difficult things I have ever done; I had to leave Daisy in the hospital and fly back to the USA, then on to England where I would be joined by Daisy who would fly, with Marie, direct from Malaysia.

Torturous Journey
Malaysia–England–USA

But Daisy grew no better. There was more pain every day. The femur had been broken. With pain medication and Marie to assist her, she endured the excruciating fourteen hour flight to London, then traveled by car more than a hundred miles to the campmeeting site.

She preached enduring intense pain. It became so severe that, after two torturous days of ministry, I urged her to return to Tulsa with Marie.

Following the campmeeting in England, we had committed ourselves to minister for a week in Sweden. So again I faced the dilemma of leaving Daisy in order to fulfill another commitment we had made.

We have always made every effort to avoid canceling engagements. We decided together that since Marie could travel with Daisy, I should go on to Sweden. She made the difficult ten hour journey to Chicago, then on to Tulsa.

Surgical Repair

Upon arrival in Tulsa, Daisy was hospitalized for examination. The bone specialist was shocked that she had been left to suffer so long. Because of muscle tension and vibration during travel, the leg was actually twisting at the breakpoint, adding to the distress. She refused surgery until I could be with her, enduring six more days of intense suffering.

As soon as I arrived home, the specialist operated, realigning the leg, affixing a six-inch steel plate to the femur to secure the alignment while the bone re-knitted. Daisy was finally able to begin her three-month recovery.

Bogota Triumph
Brazil And Hawaii

Then it was time to leave for Bogota, Colombia. Daisy was still using a cane to walk, but her courage was unbounded. She would conduct an historic Pan-American Women's Conference where thousands of women would fill the beautiful Sports Arena, and her five major books in Spanish would be presented to each participant. It was a grand success.

Then came her National Conference in Brasilia, Brazil, where she ministered to thousands of women and challenged them to be all that God had called them to be.

From there she conducted a Pacific Conference for Women in Hawaii. Most of the Pacific Rim nations were represented. It was significant.

But Daisy's lungs were in trouble. She had kept driving herself despite two recent major bouts with pneumonia — in India and in Colombia.

We were praying and believing, refusing to appease the enemy by relaxing our ministry schedules.

Before Daisy was injured in Malaysia, she had just returned from a very tough mission in Asia.

Missions Of Mercy & Faith
India—Australia

She had flown to South India to conduct a great Women's National Conference in Madras. Her hotel was located forty-five minutes by car from the conference venue.

The auditorium was stifling. The humidity was excessive. Daisy perspired as she preached.

Oscillating fans swept back and forth across the platform, and across Daisy, for ventilation. After teaching for an hour, wet with perspiration and intermittently chilled by the fans, she was crowded into a car for a forty-five minute journey to her hotel during which the air conditioner was kept at its maximum cold temperature.

This happened twice each day. Every journey added to her problem as her lungs filled with water and her body burned with fever.

Following that Madras Conference, Daisy's next engagement was scheduled for Australia. In a weakened condition, instead of resting and recuperating, she traveled to Singapore and on to Australia to conduct a National Women's Conference in Adelaide, preaching despite fever and pain in both lungs. Her courage never abated.

Then when she returned from those conferences, the national events in Bogota, Colombia, Brazil, and Hawaii were at hand. So, again, instead of resting and recovering, she proceeded to fulfill those engagements.

Penetrating Cold Rains At 8,000 Ft. Altitude

During her Bogota Conference and our Mass Miracle Crusade there, we had to cope with an untimely cold, rainy spell that swept the city for days. Daisy had been weakened by her episodes with pneumonia in India and Australia. Now she was ministering in a huge, concrete coliseum that was open, damp and cold, at an altitude of 8,000 feet where it is almost impossible for a non-acclimatized person to get warm. Her lungs filled again but she kept on preaching and ministering to the thousands of women, day after day, despite high fever. And from there, her missions to Brazil, and then to Hawaii had followed.

Daisy was a believer. She refused to yield to symptoms and kept pressing herself instead of canceling engagements and resting.

When she returned from the Pacific, in the natural, it was clear that Daisy was in very serious physical trouble.

Our next engagement was to be one of the largest Women's Conferences and Leadership Seminars we had yet planned—in Monterrey, Mexico.

Mexico's Appeal
To Build Self-Value

The pastors who came to invite us said, *"We have checked with leaders from other nations and have been told that you will lift the dignity and self-esteem of our people and preachers. We believe this is what our nation needs in order to rise up in apostolic evangelism; we believe that this will reinvigorate the Church of Mexico in her mission to our nation and to the world."*

Daisy and I had been deeply moved by this appeal and had purposed to give them our best. But she was too weakened by her bouts with pneumonia to go. It was another traumatic experience for me to have to leave her when she needed me, to go fulfill another engagement we had made. Again, Marie Brown was available to her for any need that she might have, and Karen Anaya stayed with her day and night.

The Monterrey conference was a historic success. We imported from Colombia *twenty-two tons of our books in Spanish* (five by Daisy and five by me), and presented full sets of our ten major books to all pastors, ministers, leaders, Bible School teachers and students, gospel workers, and believers who attended the conference.

I ministered, in Daisy's place, to the women of Mexico for five days. Thousands of women attended that National Women's Congress. We gave Daisy's five major books to each of the women. All lessons were recorded and those cassettes are proliferating across Latin America among the dynamic women of those nations.

Slipping Out Of My Reach

When I returned from Monterrey to Daisy's side, it was obvious that, without a miracle, she was slipping out of my reach.

Then came that dreadful and painful night when, at 2:53 a.m., the precious spirit of my lifetime sweetheart and teammate slipped away from her little body as I held her in my arms. It was the end of her earthly life with me. Her course was finished. She was with her Lord.

Chapter Eight

Return From Russia

My DAUGHTER, Pastor LaDonna, and I had ministered across Eurasia in a succession of strategic Miracle Life Conferences in the major cities of five ex-Soviet Republics.

Every day we had shared with hundreds of young Russian preachers, both men and women, whose lives and minds had been subjugated by communist ideology.

Marxist-Leninist indoctrination had demeaned the idea of God as being only a *myth*, and religion as an *opiate* — a superstition.

Following the collapse of communism, gospel ministers had begun to share Christ's message of redemption among the ex-Soviet peoples.

The young generation was responsive, eager to embrace the hope, faith, Love, and Life that the gospel gives to people.

TREASURES FOR THE EX-SOVIETS

During our Miracle Life Conferences, those hundreds of young preachers and ministers had soaked up our teaching like sponges. They had returned to their new churches and groups with new and life-changing truths to share.

Our ten major books in Russian were treasures in their hands. The truths they contained would formulate the structure for new Bible Schools and Christian training institutions.

This had been a significant mission to major areas, with two and three meetings daily, involving awkward traveling conditions, to say the least. We were tired when we arrived back in Tulsa. LaDonna had preceded me by a few days while I remained for one more conference in Moscow.

NOVOSIBIRSK TO TULSA

I began these memoirs in Novosibirsk, Siberia and I have since used every moment possible, in hotels and on planes, to record details on my laptop computer as they have come to my mind.

I had been able to cope with my loneliness during the weeks that we had been busy ministering. In fact, I felt that I had overcome some of the pathos of separation that I had suffered since Daisy's demise, and I sensed incomparable gratification for what we had witnessed in Eurasia.

The Trauma of My Return

I arrived in Tulsa late on a Sunday afternoon. Rather than to disturb Pastor LaDonna or one of our staff members on the weekend, I engaged a taxi at the airport to take me to our residence.

Upon arrival, I paid the driver, then set my suitcases through the wooden gate, into our enclosed yard. I'll never forget the wave of grief that struck me as I closed the gate and the taxi drove away. I had never felt so *alone* in my life.

I had tried to prepare myself emotionally, rationalizing that Daisy would not be there, but I had no idea that the emptiness of our residence *without her* would be so frightening and emotionally destabilizing.

The Emptiness Stunned Me

I stood there and surveyed the rose bed and the trees that Daisy and I had planted. There were the blazing red Japanese maples that she and I had enjoyed so much, and the brilliant zinnia and marigold beds — and, of course, the roses.

I pondered the beautiful blooming chrysanthemums. When we were at home, we usually kept three or four blooming plants in the house because we enjoyed flowers so much. When they would begin to wilt, I would cut back the stems and plant them. They always grew and afforded gorgeous beauty during the fall months and continued to bloom until the temperature dropped below freezing.

I walked around the house on the sidewalk where Daisy and I had so often strolled together. Everything had been manicured by the yardman to look its best when I returned. Spectacular roses were in bloom. The lawn was like a green carpet.

Daisy Was Not There

I pondered it all. *Daisy was not there.* I had always looked at that yard *with Daisy in mind.* It was *our* field of love, *our* area for recuperation, *our* garden of tranquility, *our* space for inspiration. Daisy and I had designed everything *together. But she was not there.* What did it matter now that it was so beautiful?

Angry Questions—WHY?

I felt a deep anger rise within me. *Daisy was no longer a part of ANYTHING.* WHY had she been taken from me? Without her, what was the purpose of this home—of my life? We had created an atmosphere in which we could maximize our productivity in writing and recording.

Everything had been designed *with Daisy in mind*—the roses, each tree and bush, the big sandstone boulders that we had brought from the woods. We had sat together on them, read, prayed and talked. We loved those boulders.

Now, of what value were they? *Without Daisy* they were like ghosts staring at me.

Tears flowed. I wept aloud. I groaned. I sobbed. I could not control my grief. There seemed to be no reason to continue in life or to try to be courageous. My perspective for the future was totally disoriented.

Drowning In Grief

I suddenly became aware of the psychological trauma that was destroying me. Was the real *inner*-me just now comprehending that Daisy was gone and would not be back? Had it taken a mission across Eurosia and a return to emptiness to face the devastating reality of her absence?

Had I been in psychological shock while absorbed in ministry abroad? It had been more than a year since my beloved's demise. I had purposely committed myself to as many meetings, crusades, conferences and seminars as I could sustain, believing that it would help me to avoid the subversive trauma of loneliness.

No Welcome Home

My *inner*-self seemed paralyzed—stunned when Daisy was not there to welcome me. I had worked and ministered in some of the most delicate situations that I had ever been involved in. It had been a particularly tough, but rewarding mission and I was weary. Now I had returned to our haven of love and tranquility. *But Daisy was not there*. I felt forsaken.

Almost always, we had journeyed and ministered together. At times, when ministering in the USA, I went alone. Daisy was always at the airport to meet me when I returned — ready to embrace me with her love and smiles. Those welcomes made life worth living. And I was always there to welcome Daisy when she returned from ministering somewhere.

No Reception This Time

In our missions abroad, Daisy had usually preceded me, ministering for three to six weeks preparing for our crusades. Almost always, she had arranged grand receptions for my arrival. No one will ever know the joy I felt to be met by Daisy at the airplane with her arms outstretched to receive me. We were sweethearts. Often overseas, the planes are parked away from the terminal. She always managed to obtain permission to walk out across the tarmac to receive me.

Then there would be the grand reception by thousands of national Christians whom Daisy had rallied. They would converge on the airport in trucks, lorries, and busses, on motor-cycles and bicycles, on foot and in cars.

Daisy always had a loudspeaker prepared. She would greet the people then introduce me. She was the life of the party. The people adored her charm, positive faith, and inspiring leadership.

Arrival At Entebbe
The Road Was Lined For Twenty Miles

When I arrived at the Entebbe Airport in Uganda, twenty-two kilometers from the capital city of Kampala, Daisy had met me out on the tarmac, then ushered me into the VIP lounge to meet officials, and out to the airport entry that was packed with thousands of happy people.

After our greetings and brief message to them, the parade into town began. It took us two hours to travel the twenty-two kilometers from Entebbe to Kampala. The roadway was lined with tens of thousands of people all the way into the city. We had moved slowly. Daisy and I had stood together through the open sunroof of the car, greeting the people, waving, calling to them, praying for them. Daisy planned it all. She did it in most of the cities where she prepared for our Mass Miracle Crusades.

Alone With Two Suitcases

Now, I had returned from a triumphant mission across Eurasia. *But there was no reception.* I was alone and tired, with nothing but two suitcases. The taxi had driven away. The gate had clanged shut. *Daisy was not there* — only emptiness. It was the most devastating sense of loneliness I had ever experienced.

The *"WHYS?"* bombarded me. I could not silence them. I was being swallowed by a sense of panic. *WHY come home? WHY continue to live?* It was the first time I had experienced thoughts like that. I stood there groaning out my grief, feeling so desolate — so frightened — so insecure.

Our Garden Of Eden

I realized that I had to purge those demoralizing thoughts that were poisoning me. I moved along the sidewalk to our east patio.

When I saw the beautiful pink and white patio furniture that Daisy had selected — that we had enjoyed so much together, I recalled the glorious hours we had spent there together, eating, talking, praying, reading our Bibles or mail, discussing problems or planning crusades, expressing our love. What memories!

The chairs were there but they were empty. *Daisy was not there.* She would *never* be there again. *What good were those chairs now?*

Could I ever sit there *alone* and not be grief stricken? It seemed that too much in me had died. I felt totally destabilized — terrified.

Did I Want To Go On Living?

For the first time since Daisy's demise, I didn't know if I wanted to go on living. The trauma and pathos of loneliness was too deep. *Why try to be courageous? For what? For whom?*

During the fourteen months since I had deposited her precious body at the Memorial Park between those two beautiful pines that we had planted, I had been busy, ministering, campaigning, writing, working, from early until late. Work and ministry had been my consolation—my solace—my shield.

With the passing of weeks and months, I thought I had made good progress in adjusting to life *without Daisy*. But I had been busy. Now I had returned to an empty residence. I never dreamed that the void could be so traumatic.

No One To Share My Triumphs

Negative questions assailed my mind. *WHY work so hard in Eurasia? For what? I have no one to share it with.* Before, I could share my problems or triumphs with Daisy. I loved to relive each detail with her. And when she returned from some great conference or seminar, what a pleasure it had been to sit and listen as she shared her victories with me. But now I had experienced so much, *and there was no one to share these successes with—no one to talk to.* What was the point of continuing?

It was the first time in my fourteen months of painful loneliness that I had sensed the willingness to quit living. Waves of desolate bereavement swept over me like billows.

Grace To Grow – Not Grovel

I turned to walk back around the house to retrieve my suitcases. I had not gone inside yet. I needed to unpack. I walked slowly, pondering, weeping, contemplating. I knew that I had to get my emotions under control. I had to *grow* through this experience—not wither, atrophy, or vegetate in my spirit—not grovel—not withdraw.

I reasoned within myself that separation and consequent bereavement are universal; sooner or later they become a part of life for every couple. I was aware that I would have to adapt to a different lifestyle, that I would have to *learn to live again*. My life would not be the same. The scenery would be changed. My outlook would have to be refocused. If I could summon the courage to adjust, I knew that the landscape *could* still be beautiful—there *could* be beauty if I looked for it, but, for sure, everything would be *very different*.

But I didn't want a new landscape. I wanted to keep life the way it had been before. I *chose* to be married. I loved Daisy. Our lives together were harmonious and delightful. Now I was alone. I did not want to be alone. But there was nothing that I could do about it—yet I knew that I *had* to do *something*.

Significant Lessons To Learn

Despite the pain that I was suffering, I reasoned to myself that there must be significant lessons in life to gain through an experience such as this. I wanted to observe whatever might help me to overcome the trauma and the void that I was experiencing. Then I might be able to help others who suffer loneliness or painful loss.

I thought that maybe this impact of emptiness would help my *inner*-self to come to grips with the reality that my sweetheart was gone and would not be returning. I hoped that maybe I would not suffer this shock again. Maybe something would be healed inside of me. I resolved to recover my emotional balance and to be strong. But *WHY? For whom? For what?*

I remember moving slowly, pensively back toward my suitcases. I reasoned within myself, "You thought that you built this house *for Daisy* — that you planted these gardens, flowers, trees, roses and lawn *for her*. Why did you think you were doing all of this *for Daisy?* "

Flowers, Roses, Trees—For *Whom?*

I queried myself, "Do *YOU* not cherish these flowers, these roses, these trees, this yard? You thought that you only loved them *with Daisy*. She was half of you — the *best* half. Since she came into your life at the age of seventeen, you never loved anything — *by yourself*. Nothing had value to you *alone*. Things only mattered that gave joy or meaning to you *and Daisy*."

My thoughts continued, "Now you must learn to love and enjoy and value your world *by YOURSELF*. You must discover *YOU — without Daisy*. You must ascertain what *you* enjoy, what *you* delight in, what *you* cherish, what *you* derive joy from, what gives *you* pleasure."

It Seemed Narcissistic — Sacrilegious

But this kind of logic was repugnant to me. It seemed selfish, narcissistic, even sacrilegious. To think or to speak in terms of *"me," "I," "my,"* and *"mine,"* was extrinsic, inapplicable, alien to my lifestyle and rationale. I resented the self-centeredness that these terms implied. I would have to learn a whole new way of expressing life and ministry. It had always been *"we"* and *"us"* and *"our."*

To say *"me"* and *"my"* and *"mine"* seemed egotistical and conceited. I was stunned by the implications that confronted me. Everything was shifting, being modified, altered, changed, and I was utterly helpless to recover life as I had relished it for more than a half-century.

Who Is T.L. Osborn—*Without Daisy?*

This plunged me into a deeper search. Who was T.L. Osborn—*without Daisy?* What is there in this world that really matters to him—*alone?*

I was destabilized by the discovery *that I did not know me*—the real *me.* I knew that now I must reappraise my own personhood, my life. Nothing was the same. I was a stranger to my own self. My own surroundings terrified me. I had never pondered them—*without Daisy.*

I asked myself, "Do *I* want flowers? Do *I* enjoy a garden? Am *I* interested in the news of the day? Is it of consequence for *me* to stay informed about happenings in my world? *Without Daisy,* what did things of this world matter?"

Discovering A *Different* T.L.

It was one of the greatest psychological impacts of my life to reach the age of seventy-two and to suddenly discover that I did not know T.L. Osborn—*without Daisy.* I knew the T.L. that was part of Daisy. But T.L. Osborn—*alone?* I had never known that person since he was seventeen years of age, when his whole world had been a little country farm, with some mules and cows and crops, in Oklahoma.

The T.L. Osborn of today had evolved through the experiences of a half-century of being a part of Daisy Marie Washburn. She and I had been *one*. During our lifetimes I had only constituted half of this union. *Together, we were a whole.* I only perceived life *with Daisy.* Now she was gone. I was inundated by terrifying waves of insecurity, uncertainty, apprehension. There was no one to counsel, no one with whom I could share triumphs or failures, joys or griefs.

Decision For My Future

I made a decision then and there, by my garage, standing by those suitcases: I must find out who *I* am, what *I* want—what interests *me.* This very idea seemed disgracefully selfish. I had never wanted things for *myself.* Now I knew that I must get acquainted with *my own* emotions, *my* lifestyle, the scenery along *my* road. I must perceive new hopes and new dreams for the future. I must *live*, and not die.

I know that this may sound as though I were befuddled, insecure, or unstable. Ministers of the gospel are supposed to have *answers*, not *questions.* They are expected to be steadfast—not shaken, established—not fluctuating, confident—not confused.

All that I can say is that Daisy and I had been *one* for nearly fifty-four years, and suddenly we had been ripped apart. The best part of me no longer existed. I was a half-person.

Reconstructing My Rationale

I knew that I must reappraise my life, reorganize my thoughts, reanalyse my rationale.

I knew that *I had value.* But I needed to reassess my value — *without Daisy.* I resolved to bring the surviving T.L. Osborn out into the open, and to see who *he* is, to get acquainted with *him,* to energize *him* and *his* talents, and to motivate *him* to keep the fountain of God's goodness flowing out through *him* to his hurting world.

I made up my mind that evening, to *keep on living* for the sake of millions who need God's love and *Life.*

Talking To Myself

I told myself, "T.L., it's time to take a new look at life — *through your own eyes.* Daisy is gone. Your landscape has changed. She will only be there in your memories. You must face that fact and stop grieving. You must learn to value *your* life. Your hurting world needs *you.* You must keep on communicating *your* knowledge of the gospel and *your* experiences of God's faithfulness."

I spoke to myself, "Look again at this home, these flowers, the trees, the garden, the lawn. Let *your* eyes delight in them. *You* live here. The beauty that is here now is for *you.* This is *your* Garden of Eden — a place of rest and tranquillity where *you* can be refreshed between crusades — a sanctuary where *you* can study and write truths that will bless millions of hurting people."

I reasoned, "You have work to do, ministry to accomplish, nations to reach, books to write, audio and video cassettes to record, millions of people to reach with the *Good News*."

Reconciling With Life
A Learning Experience

I told myself: "Today is a learning experience. Something is happening in you right now. You will not suffer *this* particular trauma again. The real *T.L.* is finally comprehending that *Daisy is gone*. Everything has changed. Life is different. It *can* still be beautiful, but it will be *different*."

In times of loss, there are vital lessons to learn—if one is willing to *grow* through the process of pain, instead of *grieving*. It becomes a time for a new beginning—although it is the *last* thing that one wants.

Facing a changed world, one can reassess one's inventory of life, reconsider one's priorities, refocus one's view of what is important, and reappraise one's goals.

Experiencing tragedy and loss causes one to ask many basic questions, not only about one's self, but about one's objectives in life.

Mortality Becomes More Graphic

I have learned to refocus the present moment—
this hour, this day. I have learned to avoid wast-
ing my energy in pondering my loss. The life that
remains seems more valuable than before. Mortality has become more graphic. Every remaining
day *must count for God—and for the hurting world
in which I live.*

I reminded myself, "You have experienced the
ecstasy of nearly fifty-four years of loving companionship. Be thankful for those years. Walk
courageously. Resolve to continue in life—
productively. Let your countenance project bless-
ing to people. They need you."

And the holy scriptures encouraged me: *"Lift up
the hands which hang down, and the feeble knees; And
make straight paths for your feet, lest that which is
lame be turned out of the way; let it rather be healed...
Look diligently lest you fail of the grace of God; lest
any root of bitterness spring up and trouble you..."*
He.12:12-15

Casting Down Imaginations

I knew that I was repulsing some of the inva-
sive and destructive onslaughts of grief, depression and despair that were assailing me.

I came to realize, then and there, that if my
heartache and pathos were left unconquered,
they would so demoralize me that I could die *in-*

side, then, before long, I would die physically. It was a personal crisis that I knew I must deal with.

I was *"casting down imaginations, and every high thing that exalts itself against the knowledge of God; I was bringing into captivity my thoughts to the obedience of Christ."* 2Co.10:5

I resolved that I would *continue to LIVE* by the grace and the word of God, and that I would *continue to share* His blessings with others. I would *live* for those who are living.

Daisy Triumphed
My Mission Is Not Ended

I knew that people could not draw strength from me if I allowed myself to vegetate in grief. Daisy had *finished her course* triumphantly and had gone to her reward. Her coronation had taken place. *My* mission was not over.

I resolved to hoist my shoulders, to raise my head, to lift my spirit and to savor the honor of being Christ's representative in this world.

Millions of people are suffering. I had been chosen *by Him* to bring His healing Love and compassion to humanity.

He had suffered loneliness greater than I could ever know when he prayed in the Garden of Gethsemane, *"being in an agony: and his sweat was as it were great drops of blood falling down to the ground."* Lu.22:44

LONELY—BUT NOT *ALONE*

Many times the gospels state that Christ was alone. His words in John were a comfort to me: *"I am not alone…He that sent me is with me: the Father has not left me alone."* Jn.8:16-29

When His disciples forsook Him, He knew that His Father would not leave Him. He told them: *"The hour is now come that you will be scattered…and will leave me alone: but I am not alone, because the Father is with me."* Jn.16:32

He promised, *"Lo, I am with you alway, even unto the end of the world."* Mt.28:20 He said: *"I will never leave you, nor forsake you."* He.13:5 Those promises meant more to me than ever before, and I drew courage from them.

THE MOMENT WAS SIGNIFICANT

The sun had set and it was becoming dark. I had to go inside the house. Gathering my emotional forces, I bent over to pick up my bags, resolving to embrace the lessons I had observed.

I moved cautiously because the moment was significant to my future. I knew that if I could absorb the lessons at hand, I would be stronger and this would prove to be a time of emotional healing for me.

I was weary after having traveled from Moscow, Russia, crossing ten time zones. I had been on planes for over twenty-four hours. So I told myself, "Take your bags inside. Unpack. Get some rest. Substitute *beautiful memories* for painful recollections. Treasure your golden years with Daisy. Remember that you have been blessed with more happiness than most husbands have ever known."

Tomorrow—With New Courage

The Holy Spirit comforted me. I told myself, "Tomorrow will be a new day, with new hope. The sun will rise on a new beginning that will bring new courage for living."

Jesus said, *"Seek first the kingdom of God, and His righteousness; and all these things shall be added unto you. Take no thought for tomorrow: for tomorrow shall take thought for the things of itself. Sufficient unto the day is the evil thereof."* Mt.6:33-34 And I remembered His words, *"My grace is sufficient for you."* 2Co.12:9

Something seemed to assure me that I would not suffer *this particular trauma again.* I believe God gave me the grace to *grow through my pain that evening.* Knowing of His sovereignty, I was reassured that He was in charge. But it was up to me to *"CHOOSE life and LIVE..."* Deut.30:19

God is bigger than our hurts. His incarnation in Jesus Christ brought Him to our human level where He tasted pain and suffering. He embraced the human experience. He lived on our level, grappling with the ambiguous conflicts and struggles experienced in our humanity. He was abused, rejected and condemned *on our behalf*, so that we might *LIVE*.

Jesus Understood Suffering

The writer of Hebrews admonished us to constantly *"look to Jesus, the author and finisher of our faith; who for the joy that was set before Him endured the cross, despising the shame, and is set down at the right hand of the throne of God."* He said that we should remember to *"consider Him...lest we be wearied and faint in our minds."* He.12:2-3

Jesus endured suffering and pain that is greater than we can comprehend. He descended deeper into the loneliness of despair and grief than we can imagine. *He did it for us, in our name.* God is not a sovereign being who rules from a distance. He came to our level. He tasted the grief and pain that humans experience. He laid down His life in order to lift us to rapport with Himself.

What The Incarnation Means

The wonder of the Christian message is that *God raised Christ from the dead.* And Jesus said, *"because I live, you shall live also."* Jn.14:19

His incarnation means that HE CARES FOR US—so much, in fact, that he chose to become a human and to suffer loss more terrible than we can comprehend. Regardless of how deep our pit of pain may be, we will find God there, reassuring us that He feels our hurt with us. He is not remote and detached. In our human suffering, He draws us to his bleeding side, touches us with his nail-pierced hands, heals our hurt with his loving compassion.

Reasons For Living

These are reasons why I weep during communion services. The bread and wine that represent the broken body and shed blood of Christ, remind me of His coming to my level, to bear my pain, to endure my suffering, to heal my wounds.

Not only does this comfort me in my grief; it projects *my reason to keep LIVING*. I am one of His *chosen ones*. He said, *"You have not chosen me, but I have chosen you, and ordained you, that you should go and bring forth fruit, and that your fruit should remain: that whatsoever you shall ask of the Father in my name, He may give it you."* Jn.15:16

He said, *"It behooved Christ to suffer, and to rise from the dead the third day: And that repentance and remission of sins should be preached in his name among all nations...And you are witnesses...behold, I send the promise of my Father upon you."* Lu.24:46-49

This comforts me. This is *my* mission. This had been *our* mission together—Daisy's and mine. Now it was *my* mission. *I* was still vital to God's big plan. He was still depending on *me.*

My Mission Was Clear

I had been profoundly moved by the fact that God had ENTRUSTED the gospel into our hands—now into *my* hands. Daisy could no longer journey with me and share in proclaiming Christ's message. But *I* could continue. *I* was alive. *I* knew the liberating truths of redemption. *My* mission was clear.

When the Lord came to Saul, revealing Himself to him, His message was, *"Go your way: for you are a chosen vessel for me, to bear my name before the Gentiles, and kings, and the children of Israel."* Ac.9:15 I felt that those words were for *me* now.

Chosen Vessels

Daisy and I had been *"chosen"* vessels for Him *together.* Now Daisy's *"race had been run."* Heb.12:1 She had *"fought a good fight, finished her course, and had kept the faith."* 2Ti.4:7 Jesus had welcomed her to receive the *"crown of righteousness"* with His words, *"Well done, good and faithful servant: you have been faithful over a few things, I will make you ruler over many things: enter into the joy of your Lord."* Mt.25:21 She had, like *"David, served her gen-*

eration by the will of God, and had fallen asleep, and had been laid with her foreparents..." Ac.13:36

He Has Committed The Gospel To Our Trust

But *my* race had not been completed. *I* was needed to continue the work that Jesus had *begun* Ac.1:1 and that Daisy and I had devoted fifty-three years to carry forward. He had *"COMMITTED to my TRUST the glorious gospel of the blessed God."* 1Ti.1:11 I was one of those who had been *"allowed of God to be put in TRUST with the gospel."* 1Th.2:4 Like Paul, *"the gospel...had been COMMITTED unto me."* Gal.2:7

The most inspiring fact in Christianity — the truth that infuses me with energy and courage to continue in life and ministry — *even alone*, is that God believes in us as human beings.

In fact, the Lord believes in us so completely, that He has *"committed"* His gospel into our hands. He trusts us to share it with our world. If we do not, He will not send angels to do it. God has confided His Good News into our care, choosing us, empowering us, and sending us as the interpreters of His Love.

This is awesome. This is why I cannot quit. He trusts me. *With Daisy*, I was better. But *alone*, I will do all that I can to disseminate His truth and to serve as His ambassador.

The High Position
Of Partnership With God

I think the most ennobling truth of biblical Christianity is the fact that God has *justified us*, through our faith in the sacrifice of Christ, so completely, that we are lifted to the high position of being His witnesses—His associates—His co-workers—His partners. I wish I could make the whole world understand this fact of the redemptive work of Christ.

When He assumed our guilt and bore our judgment, His vicarious intervention on our behalf was so perfect and complete that *"He brought us into the very presence of God, and we are standing there before Him with nothing left against us...the only condition being that we fully believe the Truth...convinced of the Good News that Jesus died for us, and that we never shift from trusting Him to save us."* Col.1:22-23 LB

We Now Share His Life

"God has given us a share in the very life of Christ ...and blotted out the charges proved against us...In this way He took away Satan's power to accuse us of sin, and openly displayed to the whole world Christ's triumph at the cross where our sins were all taken away." Col.2:13-15 LB *"This is the wonderful news that has come to each of us and is now spreading all over the world; And I, [T.L. Osborn,] have the joy of telling it*

to others...*So everywhere we go we talk about Christ to all who will listen...This is our work, and we can do it only because Christ's mighty energy is at work within us."* Co.1:28-29 LB These are powerful truths that give reason and purpose for living and giving and sharing the gospel of Jesus Christ with those who need Him.

In Agony, New Hope Is Born

Those verses express my commitment. This is why I have recorded this chronicle. The agonizing odyssey of my dark night of grief has been difficult. But through the knowledge of Christ's redemptive sacrifice on our behalf, new courage is born in my spirit with revived determination and purpose to *continue living.*

"For whatsoever things were written...are for our learning, that we through patience and comfort of the scriptures might have HOPE." Ro.15:4 *"Being enlightened, [I] know what is the HOPE of His calling, and the riches of the glory of His inheritance..."* Ep.1:18 God's grace gives me the courage to *"continue in the faith, grounded and settled, and [never] moved from the HOPE of the gospel."* Co.1:23

Fresh Dawn Of Discovery

With God's stimulating perspective of *LIFE*, I am able to arrive at the dawn of a fresh discovery, and to survey a new vista of *LIFE that is worth living — even without beloved Daisy, and amidst a*

179

very different landscape. I am able to stand triumphant on the summit of creative transition — blurred but not blinded, dismayed but not dissuaded, wounded but not wasted, bruised but not broken.

Returning from Russia was an ambiguous and traumatic experience. But it became a turning point for me. Being lacerated by the crisis, a balm of healing began to ameliorate my wounds. I gained in knowledge. I made vital discoveries — about *me,* and about *life.*

A Consoling Secret For Healing

My renewed perspective did not give me the answer to the "WHYS?" of Daisy's demise. It did not convince me that her departure, at the age of only seventy, was good or right. It did not expunge my grief or loneliness. The vacuum still haunts me.

But God unveiled to me a consoling and healing secret for triumphing over the devastation of despair. By refocusing memory *positively* instead of *remorsefully*, tragedy could be transcended, LIFE could continue to be worth living — *even in change,* and a renewed perspective could mean vital and productive growth for my life in resolving to continue living for the good of others.

Chapter Nine

God's Message
In The Flowers

Soon AFTER RETURNING from Russia, I had to travel back across the Atlantic to minister at the Ulf Eckman Campmeeting in Uppsala, Sweden. Two weeks after that I would minister at the Peter Gammons Campmeeting in England and then fly back across Scandinavia to minister for a week in Helsinki, Finland where thousands would jam the big Ice Arena daily.

Between Sweden and England, my option was to return to Tulsa for two weeks, or to stay in Europe. Since I had my laptop computer with me, I could work on projects that were urgent, so I chose to spend those two weeks in the village of Thirsk, England.

During the last two years of Daisy's life, we had worked together—as much as we could, preparing an *Anthology and History of our World Ministry*. It comprises twenty-three huge volumes, each containing about a thousand pages — plus an *Index* volume of several hundred pages. Our plan has been to place this historic *24-Volume Collection* in universities and leading Bible schools around the world.

Imagine what a witness these twenty-four big red volumes will be in the ex-Soviet Union. Our lives spanned the same years that Leninist doctrine prevailed in Russia. This *unique* collection will be a record of what God has been doing in seventy-four nations, during the same years that communism was insisting that He did not exist.

Sections of those volumes that Daisy and I had been writing were on my computer hard disk. We had not been able to finalize them, so I thought the quiet village of Thirsk would be a good place to complete several sections of the work.

Two Weeks Of Self-Discovery

I installed myself in the quaint but picturesque *Golden Fleece Hotel,* Market Place, Thirsk, North Yorkshire. I was able to book Room 4 where the sun shined in through a rather large window overlooking the village town square.

In the mornings and evenings, I would go out for long walks. There were many pathways and sidewalks in the residential areas. The British people love to walk. I was fascinated by their manicured cottage gardens and by the beauty of their roses and flowers.

I was captivated by the wall mounted flower boxes, hanging flower pots, standing boxes and every shape and style of flower containers meticulously arranged in every available space around entryways and on cottage walls.

Flowers At Tulsa—In England

I reflected on my trauma concerning our rose beds and flowers in Tulsa, following Daisy's demise. We always had rose beds which I tended with great care *because Daisy loved roses*. I tried to always keep bouquets in our kitchen, living room, bedroom and even bathroom when we were home.

I enjoyed going out in the mornings to cut roses, bringing them in, trimming the stems and arranging them in our collection of vases. Daisy always added finishing touches and lovingly placed them about in our house. She would smell each rose that I had cut, offering me kisses and gestures of love.

What Good Is A *ROSE—Without LOVE*

But *after Daisy died*, I had walked out onto our patio, bordered by a special rosebed, and had been emotionally stunned by the thought: *What good is a ROSE without LOVE?* That notion haunted me for weeks.

My life felt like a concert hall without music;

... a song without lyrics;

... a rainbow without color;

... a flagpole without a flag;

... an opera without a voice;

... a bird without a song;

... a sky without a star;

... a piano without a keyboard;

... a harp without a string;

... a studio without a sound;

... a face without a smile;

... a violin without a bow;

... a lamp without a light;

... a frame without a picture;

... a fireplace without a fire;

... an existence without a life.

What good is a ROSE without LOVE...without DAISY?

I walked among those neat little British cottages in Thirsk, England, admiring the luxuriant flower gardens and the hanging flower baskets spilling their kaleidoscopic array of opulent blossoms. I paused often; I reminisced; I wept by myself there along those pathways.

I remembered the times that Daisy and I had meandered by our flower gardens, drawing inspiration from the tranquil atmosphere, dreaming dreams together, planning ministry events, conceiving ideas for books and Bible courses, for crusades and conferences.

Provoking Questions
Learning About T.L.

I began to ask myself: "Why are you so attracted by the flowers and the charm of these English gardens? Pondering their splendor is bringing back a thousand memories of you and Daisy together. Is this good for you?"

I began to observe something about myself — about T.L. *without Daisy*. For fifteen lonely months, I had been struggling to get acquainted with ME — *without Daisy*. Since her demise, I had not been able to tend our roses. They made her absence too vivid because they bespoke our love and life together. I felt that I could never grow roses or hang flowers on our patios again.

Our Hanging Gardens

On both our east and west patios, I had arranged hooks along the overhanging beams. Each spring, I would hang a dozen bright red, pink and lavender geranium and begonia baskets so that our patios were like hanging gardens. I had not been able to hang a single flower basket since my sweetheart had departed.

Again and again, as I tried to recoup from grief and despair, I asked myself, "Who am I? Do *I* like flowers? Do flowers bring *ME* joy? Or did I just hang them there *for Daisy?*"

Who Was T.L. *Without Daisy?*

There I was, walking among the cottages of a quaint little English village, drawing inspiration from each blossom. I suddenly realized that I was discovering something about T.L. Osborn, the man whom I did not know — *alone.*

I leaned over the little fences or neat stone walls there in Thirsk to touch the blossoms. I savored the rich aroma of the roses. Their fragrance made me sense Daisy. It was like a visit with her. She seemed to be with me.

God's Grace Displayed For *Me*

But I was making a discovery about *me. I* loved flowers. *ME! — I loved them. I* drew strength and inspiration from their beauty. They were displaying the graces and beauty of God — *to ME.* They were God's gift *to ME.*

God was reaching out to me through each blossom, reminding me: "I love *YOU*, T.L. My grace is abundant toward *YOU*. I am here with beauty and fragrance, with form and glory, for *YOU*. Life around *YOU* is beautiful—always. Don't miss it. You are learning to walk alone—without Daisy. I am with *YOU*. *I will never leave you nor forsake you.* Don't miss MY presence, MY glory, MY loveliness, MY companionship."

I realized that I was discovering *ME*—the real T.L. And I was embracing the presence of God and of His love for *me* in a new way. I was realizing how much *I* loved beauty and fragrance and that it all bespoke God's love—for *ME*. I felt sublime waves of healing love penetrating me through those flowers. *They were giving me messages of love—from God.*

"I Will Plant Roses Again!"

I made a decision there in the village of Thirsk, England. I told myself,

"Next spring, I will plant roses again.* I will hang geraniums and begonias again. I will surround myself with flowers, and they will express the fragrance and beauty of nearly fifty-four years with my sweetheart."

---

* In April of 1997—two years after Daisy's demise, I planted a beautiful rosebed and hung geraniums and begonias on my patios. I did it to commemorate our wedding on April 5, 1942. Those flowers inspire memories of Daisy, and their fragrance is a witness of God's unfailing presence in my life.

And I assured myself, *"Those flowers that I shall hang and plant will not only remind me of my years with Daisy. They will bespeak God's love and care and presence with ME, new and fresh every morning."*

Blossoms Will Bloom Again
Birds Will Sing To Me Again

I projected: I will rise early each day. The flowers will inspire me again while I exercise. The birds will sing their fresh songs to me. And when the weather is nice, I will eat my plate of fresh fruit, or my noon salad, under the hanging geraniums and begonias again. I will read my French and my Spanish Bibles amidst their beauty. And I will kneel and pray, looking up through the blossoms and the colors and I will be strengthened by Him who will *"never leave me nor forsake me."Heb.13:5*

I discovered in England that life *could* continue to be beautiful for me. I had not spent my life planting and cultivating roses *just for Daisy.* I had done it *for me too.* And I decided that T.L. Osborn was a nice fellow—*himself;* that I could learn to like him and to enjoy living with him because he is a gentle person, a believer.

I knew that he could continue living and loving and ministering to a hurting world because the fragrance and the love of God would continue to flow through him to needy people.

My days in Thirsk, England, were days of inward healing, of great consolation — and of new resolve. Jesus spoke of *"the lilies of the field"* Mt.6:28 to emphasize how much God cares for us.

The Rod That *Bloomed Blossoms*

In Hebrew history, when God wanted to reconfirm his call upon His servant Aaron, *"behold, the rod of Aaron brought forth buds, and bloomed blossoms."* Nu.17:8 Their color and beauty reaffirmed God's anointing upon the one He had chosen.

I knew that God had spoken to me through those blossoms in England. The fragrance and beauty of new roses, geraniums and begonias at my dwelling would reaffirm His anointing and calling upon my life, too.

The Spirit of God in Isaiah brought forth a message of new hope and new life for *"the wilderness and the solitary place."* I had felt like I had been in a deserted, solitary place, *alone.*

The prophet said, *"the desert would rejoice, and blossom as the rose; that it would blossom ABUNDANTLY, and rejoice with joy and singing."* Is.35:1-2 I felt the Lord was speaking to me. *My desert would blossom again.*

I knew that if I was blessed, others would be blessed. If I was healed, others would be healed. God's message encouraged me. It refocused my life and lifted me from painful bereavement to a new beginning.

Mission Defined
Miracles—Songs—Everlasting Joy

Isaiah's words in chapter 35 were, *"See the glory of the Lord, and the excellency of our God. Strengthen the weak hands, and confirm the feeble knees. Say to them that are of a fearful heart, Be strong, fear not: behold your God …will come and save you."*

His message to me continued, *"The eyes of the blind shall be opened, and the ears of the deaf shall be unstopped. The lame shall leap as an hart, and the tongue of the dumb shall sing: for in the wilderness, waters shall break out, and there will be streams in the desert….The ransomed of the Lord shall come with songs and everlasting joy; they shall obtain joy and gladness, and sorrow and sighing shall flee away."*
Isa.35

My Desert Would Blossom Abundantly

God was reviving me and renewing His Life in me with courage to embrace a new lifestyle, to lift up my eyes, to hoist my shoulders, and to keep reaching out to my world with the message of His Love.

My life would no longer be a *desert;* it would *"blossom like the rose — and blossom abundantly…with joy and singing and glory."*

Healing For The Brokenhearted Oil Of Joy For Mourning

Fresh purpose for living welled up inside me. I knew God had sent His Spirit upon me to *"preach the gospel to the poor; and to heal the brokenhearted."* Lu.4:18 He was ministering to *me.* I had been walking through a long and lonely valley. My heart had been broken. I had mourned.

But I knew that He *"gives...the oil of joy for mourning, the garment of praise for the spirit of heaviness; because [He wanted] me to be called a tree of righteousness, planted by the Lord, that He might be glorified."* Is.61:3

I knew that He had *"redeemed my life from [the] destruction [of loneliness and grief]; He had crowned me with lovingkindness and tender mercies."* Ps.103:4 In the midst of my valley, He was manifesting His love. Healing was taking place inside me. A fresh courage to keep on living and ministering in my hurting world was beginning to be felt. The Lord, my Shepherd, was *"restoring my soul...leading me beside still waters...He was with me; His rod and His staff were giving me comfort."* Psa.23

I felt like David when he prayed, *"Lord, let your tender mercies come to me, THAT I MAY LIVE."* Ps.119:77 I knew that He is *"the rose of Sharon, and the lily of the valleys;"* Song.2:1 that He is *"altogether lovely."* Song 5:16

Chapter Ten

The Monument
The Epitaph

DAISY'S FATHER, and mine, though very poor, had both purchased family lots in the local cemeteries of their communities—hers at Merced, California, and mine at Pawnee, Oklahoma. She and I were taught that parents should make preparations for their eventual demise and burial so that friends and family would not have those decisions imposed upon them.

As we advanced in years, we decided to do as our families had done—and as Abraham and Sarah had done. *Ge.25:10*

For forty years, we had driven through the Memorial Park Cemetery where our infant daughter, Mary Elizabeth, and our evangelist son, T.L. Jr., had been interred.

One day we selected and bought Lot 69 of Section 5, Skyview South.

Planning A Final Statement

While reading the Bible together, we had noticed that Abraham *"set a pillar"* Ge.35:20 on the *"buryingplace"* that he and Sarah had bought. So, again, we followed their example. We ordered a granite stone. Our lives had been lived orderly. We wanted our demise to be the same.

Then we needed to plan words for an *Epitaph — a final statement of our lives.* It would be engraved on the face of the stone. We chose words that would remind passers-by of Christ's commission and of our commitment to it. We hoped to motivate others to think about God's purpose in their lives too.

The monument designer knew of our world ministry and suggested an etching of Daisy and me, walking hand-in-hand across the world.

A Psalm And Words From Christ

We selected a statement from the Psalms: "WE HAVE PREACHED RIGHTEOUSNESS IN THE GREAT CONGREGATIONS...WE HAVE DECLARED THY SALVATION"...AMONG THE NATIONS.Psa.40:9-10 (We added the last three words.) Two other Bible verses were inscribed : "THE SEED IS THE WORD OF GOD," Luke 8:11 "THE FIELD IS THE WORLD." Mat.13:38 For the reverse side, we chose Christ's words, "GO YE INTO ALL THE WORLD AND PREACH THE GOSPEL TO EVERY CREATURE." Mark 16:15

These objectives were the focus of Dr. Daisy's life and ministry for more than a half-century.

- ◆ Find a need and meet it.
- ◆ Find a hurt and heal it.
- ◆ Find someone down and lift them up.
- ◆ Find despair and introduce hope.
- ◆ Find confusion and transpose order.
- ◆ Find hopelessness and minister faith.
- ◆ Find mediocrity and seed excellence.
- ◆ Find broken lives and motivate renewal.
- ◆ Find distress and render comfort.
- ◆ Find rejection and communicate LOVE.

Memorial Park Cemetery, Sect. 5, Skyview South, Lot 69, E. 51 St. at Memorial Dr., Tulsa, OK

T.L. says he has stood by his wife's grave and asked: "How could we have better invested ourselves as a husband-wife team? How could our years together have been more productive for the Kingdom of God? What greater reward could we have possibly striven together for than that of bringing human persons into *"God's Kingdom of righteousness and peace and joy?"* Rom. 14:17

Two Pines To Depict Our Two Lives

Although the words were commemorative, the monument would be cold and bespeak *mortality*. We wanted something *LIVING*. We both loved to plant trees so we decided to transplant two nice pines at the site, one on the east and one on the southwest edges of the plot to give shade and *life*.

I went into the countryside and located two unusual pines in an abandoned tree-farm by a river. Covered by overgrowth, they had been unnoticed. I cut through the weeds and brush and discovered that they were distinct in shape and ideal for what we wanted.

I pruned them to enhance their unique contours, then a friend balled them, transported them to the park and planted them for us. They are beautiful.

Shade For The Day
Green For All Seasons

The east tree has two flat layers of limbs because its top had been clipped earlier to stunt its vertical growth. The branches had spread horizontally — heavy in one direction. We positioned it where its extended limbs would eventually provide shade from the morning sun.

The southwest pine has curved branches (unusual for the Japanese Black species). We positioned it so the limbs would sweep down toward the plot providing afternoon shade.

Something Beautiful To Represent *LIFE*

We had created something beautiful — to represent *Life in all seasons.*

We wanted two trees to represent the two of us as lifetime teammates in ministry. Being different in shape, they express our uniqueness; being of the same species, they depict our unity; being evergreens, they represent God's faithfulness and our commitment *"in season and out of season."* 2Ti.4:2

CHAPTER ELEVEN

DAISY'S LEGACY

DAISY AND I had devoted our lives in ministry together to multitudes in nations around the world. She had invested so much of her best in making long and arduous journeys abroad to prepare and to organize our mass crusades of evangelism. She had toiled relentlessly to make each crusade a success—never complaining but always exuding cheer and faith and courage.

She had negotiated with national customs officers, effecting duty-free entry of huge shipments of *Tools for Evangelism* and great stockpiles of literature in the languages of the people.

Now *Daisy was gone.* There at her buryingplace in Tulsa, I would stand and ponder the millions of miles she had journeyed to bring hope, love, and life to those in despair. Had it been worth it? Did anyone care about the enormous work she had done?

Our Registered Objective

Back in 1949, at the institution of our missionary organization, we registered our life's objective: *To Express And Propagate The Gospel Of Jesus Christ To All People Throughout The World.* We had invested our lives to carry out that mission.

Now Daisy's life was ended. I stood there alone, reading the words of our epitaph. Had our passion and drive maybe shortened her life?

She could have stayed home and enjoyed so much of life. Was I to blame that her beautiful life had ended too soon?

The Epitaph That Haunted Me

The words of our epitaph had haunted me, mocked me, accused me. Daisy had been brave. We had given our best to minister God's love to forgotten millions.

As I stood there, pondering the words that we had conceived as our final statement together, I knew that there were more forgotten millions than when we had begun. Had our commitment mattered? Had Daisy's tenacity and devotion that drove her in the tough and demanding details of this world ministry been too strenuous for her?

I would sense waves of bitterness sweeping over me like ugly layers of invading, toxic smog.

Now my sweetheart and teammate was *gone*. I was left *alone*. Her precious little body was lying there. What did those grandiose words matter now: "WE HAVE PREACHED RIGHTEOUSNESS TO THE GREAT CONGREGATIONS...WE HAVE DECLARED THY SALVATION"...TO THE NATIONS.

DISCOURAGEMENT & DEMORALIZATION THE HARVEST OF NEGATIVE THINKING

Time after time, I stood there alone near Daisy's body and struggled with the issues of life. I did not want to be negative. I was trying to come to grips with the imposing realities I faced.

I knew that discouragement was produced by negative thoughts that could be psychologically fatal to me. I had often taught that we cannot help what happens to us but that we have absolute control over our reactions to those events. Now I had to practice what I had preached and nothing in me wanted to rise to the challenge.

DEFEATING THE DEMONS

To defeat the demons of paralyzing negativism, loneliness and panic that repeatedly tried to sap the strength and courage out of my life, I decided to draw a line and to repulse that smothering cloud of diabolical despair that obscured my vision of the new vista God wanted me to perceive.

I stood between those two beautiful pines that guarded over Daisy like faithful sentinels. I knew that I must not permit Satan's depression to demoralize me further. *I had to reverse the order of my thinking.* I did not *want* to. It was not easy. But I realized that I *must* take charge of my thoughts.

I began to ask *BETTER* questions: "What purpose could be nobler and more worthwhile than that for which we had given our lives *together*? How could we have better invested our years? How could we have been more productive in the Kingdom of God? What greater reward could we have striven for than that of bringing human persons into *'God's Kingdom of righteousness and peace and joy?'"* Ro.14:17

Obeying Christ

Daisy and I had specifically obeyed what Christ had told His followers to do. He had said, *"If you continue in my word, then are you truly my disciples."* Jn.8:31 We had done that. He had asked, *"Why call me Lord, and do not the things which I say?"* Lu.6:46 Then He had emphasized that *"hearing His word and DOING it was building one's house on a sure foundation."* Lu.4:47-48(Paraphrased) We had heard His word, and we had acted on it. Our foundation had been solid.

Our ministry together had given hope, faith, courage, love, and *LIFE* to millions.

"You Saved My Life"

I remembered how thousands of people had spoken or written to us expressing that they had been saved and brought to the knowledge of Christ through our ministries.

Innumerable times people had said or had written, *"You saved my life!" "I got saved in your crusade." "I was healed of an incurable disease when you prayed." "My life was transformed when I heard you proclaim the gospel." "I was a nobody when you came; now I have discovered my value. God loves me. He works through me. I am His representative now."*

I pondered the miraculous transformations of hundreds of thousands of lives in nations worldwide. There could be no doubt: *Ours had been the highest and noblest purposes to which any couple could commit their lives. No other mission or target could possibly compare.*

We humans are social beings. Our lives are a part of other lives. If we are objective in life, we will involve ourselves in some way to help other people. Daisy and I had done that — *together.*

Life's Mission Of Mercy

So often we had repeated the common success adage — and had added to it:

Find a need and meet it.
Find a hurt and heal it.

201

Find someone down and lift them up.
Find despair and introduce hope.
Find confusion and transpose order.
Find hopelessness and minister faith.
Find mediocrity and seed excellence.
Find broken lives and motivate renewal.
Find distress and render comfort.
Find rejection and communicate LOVE.

Those noble objectives had constituted the focus of our ministries for more than a half-century.

Suppose...Just Suppose...

Standing there at Daisy's grave, I contemplated our years together and how they *might* have been.

Suppose we had given ourselves to build and permanently pastor a great church. (We had pastored three churches and had enjoyed great success and church growth each time.)

But, I reasoned, "The best and the most that any devoted pastor can accomplish is to give people hope and faith and love that breed a God-life here on earth."

That is what Daisy and I had done together — and we had brought those virtues to innumerable families, villages, towns, cities, provinces, and nations around the world. That had been the consuming passion of our lives. Jesus had died *for the world.* Our mission had been to *tell the world.*

Millions Of Believers
Thousands Of Preachers

Today, there are millions of gospel believers and thousands of preachers who have been saved and guided into new hope and faith and love, through our crusades or seminars or tracts or audio and video cassettes, produced and provided for them, *without cost*, in their languages.

We had provided scores of four-wheel drive vehicles for gospel promulgation, which had facilitated bringing new beginnings and a higher lifestyle to the precious peoples of thousands of previously UNreached villages and towns.

We had published hundreds of tons of our gospel literature in one hundred and thirty-two languages and had provided it *free* for Christian witnessing worldwide.

Thirty Thousand
National Missionaries

We had sponsored *over thirty thousand national preachers as full-time missionaries* to UNreached tribes, villages and areas of the world.

Thousands of new churches had been established and had become self-supporting through their ministries.

We had affected fundamental changes in world evangelism and world missionary policies, and had inaugurated and sustained many other vast world outreaches.

Among the millions of new converts resulting from these global programs of gospel evangelism, there are tens of thousands who have become evangelists, pastors, teachers, preachers and ministers of *Good News* to other millions.

THE *BEST* INVESTMENT

Yes, standing there by Daisy's buryingplace, I reassured myself that *the purposes to which we had devoted nearly fifty-four years of ministry together spelled LIFE WORTH LIVING!*

This reappraisal of our lives together helped me. It reconfirmed to me that Daisy and I had invested our years together *in the most worthy and rewarding ministry possible for followers of Christ*—saving lives from despair, hopelessness, disease, sin and death—mostly lives that would have otherwise been UNreached, UNloved, UNtouched, UNcared for, UNproductive.

Satan wanted to obscure these facts. But as I pondered them there at Daisy's grave, I stood taller and prouder (or more gratified) knowing that my lifetime associate-minister and teammate *had not lived in vain.* Her life—a good life, a fulfilled life of nearly seventy-one years—had marked millions of other lives with the gospel of Christ's immeasurable Love.

Dignity For Those Who Are Ignored

I thought of the hopelessness and despair among the ignored women of the world, victims of religions (Christian and pagan alike) that have imposed upon them doctrines of second-rate citizenship, pontificating that they are unworthy to proclaim Christ's message or to represent Him in public ministry.

It seemed that I could hear Daisy saying what she had announced so many times, *"I am a voice announcing that your redemption is come, that your redeemer is here, that your emancipation has been declared, that your ransom is paid; and I am announcing it boldly to women and men of all colors, classes, races, and nationalities."*

As I stood there, I could hear the echo of her statement, *"There are some things that are wrong about religion, that deprecate women, and I intend to see that those things are changed."*

Seeding For Change

What gratification swelled inside me as I reflected upon so much that she had accomplished to *change some things!* The *seeds* of truth that she sowed are procreating themselves worldwide, and as a result, women are discovering their *identity*, their *equality*, their *dignity*, and their *destiny in God's plan of redemption*. Daisy often said:

"We cannot actually change things; we can only *SEED FOR CHANGE.*" That is a profound truth.

I wept with joy as I pondered the tons of her five major books that are bringing truth to women—and to men, around the world: *The Woman Believer, Woman Without Limits, Women And Self-Esteem, Five Choices For Women Who Win,* and *New Life For Women.* I thought of her remarkable Bible Courses being used in Bible Schools and churches worldwide.

I knew how much she believed that *"there is neither Jew nor Greek, neither bond nor free, neither male nor female: for we are all one in Christ Jesus."* Ga.3:28

Rediscovery For Multitudes

I pondered the international influence of Daisy's ministry through her Women's National Seminars and Conferences.

I thought of one of her recent conferences where over five thousand women attended. Among them was a woman, seventy years of age. Her teeth were gone, and she had nothing but a Bible and an old bicycle.

She told Dr. Daisy that she had raised up seven churches in seven villages. She explained that if God had given more days in the week, she could have had more churches. She dedicated one day per week to ministry in each village.

That old woman had attended our crusade two years earlier—*just two years earlier*. She had never known that God's Holy Spirit would anoint and bless a *woman* in ministry the same as a man.

When she saw Dr. Daisy preaching to a multitude of people and witnessed the mighty miracles of healing that took place when Daisy prayed for the multitude, it revolutionized that woman's life. She said, if God can use *that* woman, He can use *me*. Hundreds of women, in towns and villages around the globe have reached that same conclusion.

Standing there at Daisy's grave, wiping tears, I imagined telling her, *"Darling, your daughter and I have scattered your five major books in over 600 villages and towns of the ex-Soviet Union. Women all across those Republics are now discovering themselves in Christ through the legacy of your books."*

I wanted to tell her, *"Those thousands of witnesses are continuing to labor in the harvest—while you 'rest from your labors.'"* And I would add, *"We are translating them into Polish now, and will soon sow your writings in conferences all across Poland, and many more nations."*

The Epitaph No Longer Chides Me

Our epitaph no longer scoffed at me. *I had defeated the demons of demoralization.*

Today, when I stand there between those beautiful pines, I feel a sense of pride. I read our epitaph and I scorn the devil who hates what Daisy accomplished — *and what her seed is continuing to produce in nations around the world.*

Making A Better World

Yes, Daisy and I were wise in our final statement together:

"WE HAVE PREACHED RIGHTEOUSNESS TO THE GREAT CONGREGATIONS...WE HAVE DECLARED THY SALVATION"...TO THE NATIONS.

We have sown the *"seed of God's Word"*Lu.8:11 in the *"field of the world."*Mt.13:38

Our lives together have made a vast difference. Our world is better. Millions are saved and transformed, and thousands of them are carrying the message of God's salvation to other millions.

Daisy's *LEGACY*

What a legacy Daisy has left to women, and to men, in so many nations of the world! It is a legacy *IN FLESH AND BLOOD*, exhibited in the lives of those who have embraced Christ and who, because of her influence, are communicating His love to others. They are the carriers of the seed for this generation.

When Jesus returned to the Father, He left no institution that bore His name, but He left *MEN AND WOMEN* who had become His followers and who were committed to *"go into all the world and to preach the gospel to every creature."* Mk.16:15 His legacy was *IN PEOPLE*.

The Father revealed Himself *in flesh.* Jn.1:14 Then Christ's message was committed to those who followed Him. They communicated it to succeeding generations. Daisy gave her life to transmit it to millions of *her* generation. Now *they* have become His witnesses, so she continues to minister through them. The seed procreates itself. *Something of Daisy keeps on living through those who have been enlightened by her ministry. That is her Legacy — PEOPLE.*

Triumphant Coronation

There is no way that one's life can have a greater coronation than to influence others to embrace Christ, and then to finish one's course and to rest in peace. That constitutes *Ultimate Triumph.* John said, *"Blessed are the dead which die in the Lord...that they may rest from their labors; and their works do follow them."* Re.14:13

One day, standing there at Daisy's grave, I thought, "Suppose we had lived our lives at home, in a beautiful environment; suppose I had been involved in a secular business and Daisy in some career of her own?

"Suppose we had been scientists or professors in some college or university, or lawyers, or heads of companies that offered worthy services or products?

"What would the end result have been of those enterprises or vocations? Would it not have been *to make life better or more successful or happier for people?*"

That is what we gave our lives together for, and we have made that possible *for millions who had no one else to offer them help.*

We devoted our best to filling the most desperate of human needs, the need to discover peace with God and to embrace Christ as Savior. *No secular career on earth can offer more joyous fulfillment than what we have experienced together.*

Ultimate Success

Daisy is in heaven now. We were together more than most couples are privileged to be. We loved, romanced, ate, planned, traveled, studied, discovered, served and ministered TOGETHER.

Could any couple, in any professional career, have enjoyed more of life together than we have savored?

So often Daisy and I had talked about our commitment to the task of World Evangelization. We had always believed that this was the work nearest the heart of God because *"He so loved THE WORLD, that He gave His only begotten Son, that whosoever believeth in Him should not perish, but have everlasting life.* Jn.3:16

Daisy and I endorsed the question that the great missionary stateman, Oswald J. Smith, had posed: *"Why should anyone hear the gospel twice before everyone has heard it once?"*

We had always resolved that if we had other lives to live, we would live them as we have lived the years God granted to us together, *ministering His love in our hurting world.*

From their youth (above) Daisy and T.L. have ministered as a team. Here, during one of their first gospel tent crusades in Pennsylvania, they display a collection of discarded crutches, braces and other aids as proof that God confirms their preaching with *"signs and wonders."*

Daisy Osborn ministers the gospel to the multitudes who attend the Osborn mass crusades in the Javanese cities of Djakarta and Surabaya, Indonesia.

Dr. Daisy's ministry touched millions of women and men worldwide. She gave of herself, of her time, of her abilities, and of her talents to minister God's love in her hurting world, lifting people from despair to God's best.

Daisy said, "I have discovered that Jesus is in people. In a very real sense, as I minister to the needs and the hurts of *'one of the least of these,'* I am *ministering to Him."* (Top: Asia. Center: Africa. Bottom: Latin America.)

Whether one-by-one, group-by-group, or nation-by-nation, the multi-national gospel ministry of Dr. Daisy Osborn has inspired women and men alike to discover true dignity, peace and happiness in the non-judgmental role of Christ's love-representatives. Here she engages a group of university students, on the steps of the Buddhist Marble Temple in Bangkok, Thailand, and witnesses to them about Jesus Christ.

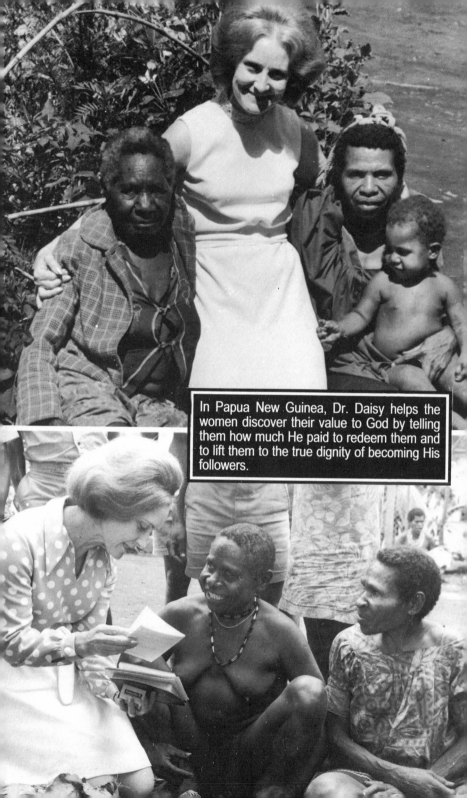

In Papua New Guinea, Dr. Daisy helps the women discover their value to God by telling them how much He paid to redeem them and to lift them to the true dignity of becoming His followers.

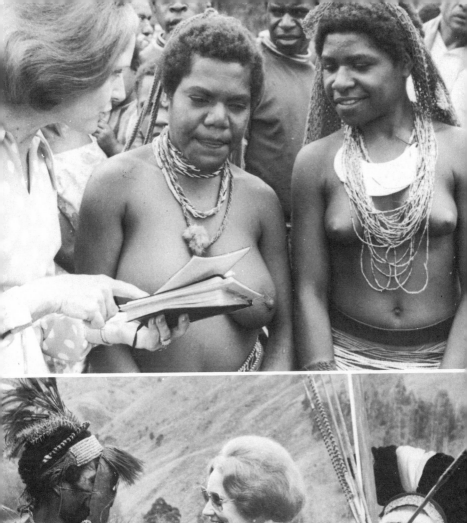

LOVE does not see traditional and cultural barriers. Love sees the person of this Pokot tribeswoman, the Buddhist nun and the Buddhist monk (opposite page) with all of whom Dr. Daisy has shared the message of Christ.

WHEREVER Daisy journeys in her worldwide gospel missions, she shares Christ and His love — with a Buddhist nun (top) and a Buddhist monk.

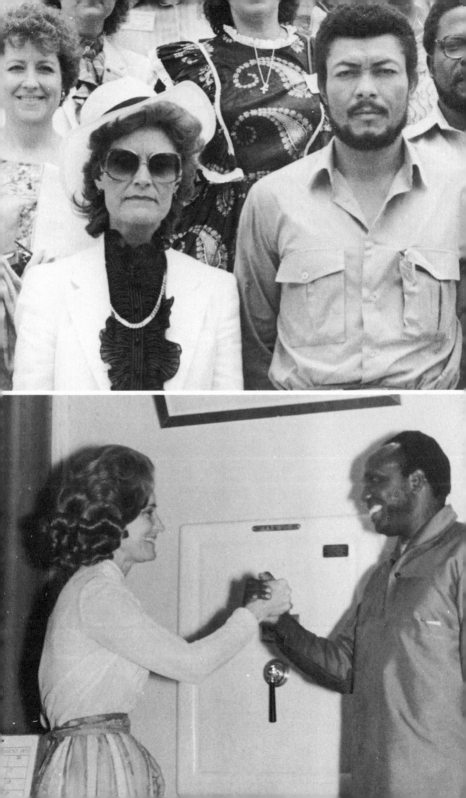

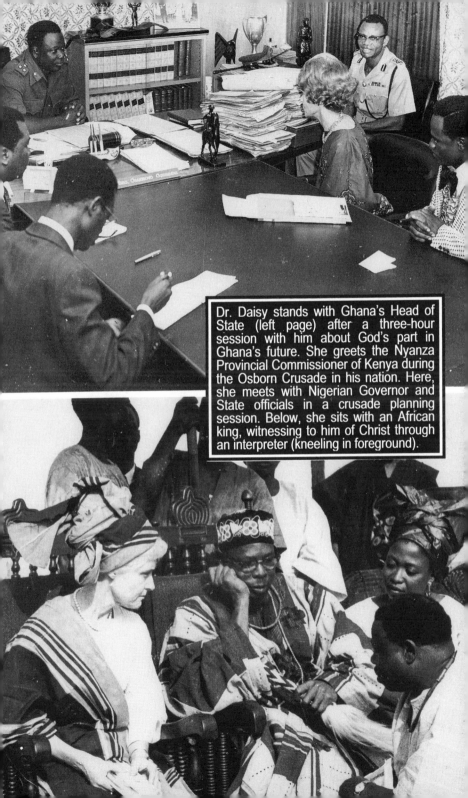

Dr. Daisy stands with Ghana's Head of State (left page) after a three-hour session with him about God's part in Ghana's future. She greets the Nyanza Provincial Commissioner of Kenya during the Osborn Crusade in his nation. Here, she meets with Nigerian Governor and State officials in a crusade planning session. Below, she sits with an African king, witnessing to him of Christ through an interpreter (kneeling in foreground).

Dr. Daisy Osborn, international gospel diplomat and ambassador, with the President of Kenya and with Nigerian Catholic bishop (opposite page), with Bendal State Governor and Chief of Police, and with President of the Philippines.

In Ghana, a desperate mother thrust her dead baby into Daisy's arms. Sensing God's will to show His power to the mother, she held the tiny corpse and prayed. Then she commanded death to release the child and its life was restored by a miracle.

Daisy always believed °that her mission in life was to bring Christ and His life to people—accessible, embraceable, tangible.

Daisy Osborn, a dynamic preacher of hope and courage, always inspired both women and men to believe the gospel and to follow Jesus Christ. Throngs heard her daily at the Municipal Stadium Grounds in Mombasa, Kenya.

As Dr. Daisy ministered in Mombasa, the multitude was like the people in Samaria who *"with one accord gave heed to those things which [she] spoke, hearing and seeing the miracles which [were wrought]."* Ac.8:6

Dr. Daisy Osborn's National Women's Miracle Day Rally at stadium field in Surabaya, Java, Indonesia.

Dr. Daisy addresses a multitude of women at her Java National Women's Day Rally in Surabaya, Java. Thousands are lifted to new levels of self-esteem and to new faith in Jesus Christ during this historic and pace-setting amassment of Indonesian women. Their lives can never be the same again.

Here, Dr. Daisy conducts a pace-setting National Women's Day Celebration at the Capital city of Kampala, Uganda, with well over

Daisy shares Bible ministry secrets with thousands of African women at the Osborns' National Women's Ministry Seminar in Kenya's Nyanza Province.

After meeting Ghana's Head of State, and addressing the nation by television, Dr. Daisy conducts a National Women's

00,000 women present—besides the men and children. Dr. Daisy's example has given courage to hundreds of Ugandan women who are oday in full time ministry, evangelizing and forming new churches.

Conference at the capital city of Accra, Ghana, West Africa. Distinguished women from several nations journeyed to Ghana for this historic event.

Women's National Conference—E. Africa

Daisy Osborn seeds the women of the world in her national women's events abroad, sharing with them strategic biblical insight concerning their identity, dignity, equality and destiny in God's redemptive plan.

Indonesian Women's Day—Surabaya, Java, Indonesia

Women's National Miracle Day—Kampala, Uganda

Australian Conference

Dr. Daisy always believed that the most important achievement in life is to bring the miracle gospel of Jesus Christ to people, as she does here to a multitude in East Africa. Insets: She rejoices with a Moslem man who has been blind, a Hindu lady who was a deaf-mute since birth, and an African man—all miraculously healed as she proclaimed the miracle-working power of the gospel of Christ.

Dr. Daisy preaches ...at Women's Conference—Nigeria

...at Osborns' Soulwinning Institute—Kenya

...at World Missions Convention—Norway

...at National Women's Conference—USA

Daisy gives keynote address at her National Conference in Adelaide, Australia.

The Osborn daughter, LaDonna, preaches at *Int'l Gospel Center* at Tulsa, OK where she is the senior pastor-overseer.

Dr. Daisy says, "Jesus is the recipient of everything that we do for people." Here she shares Christ's love with a woman in Thailand.

Dr. Daisy arrives on location to set into motion another apostolic mission of gospel ministry.

WELCOME BA__ ___ DAISY OSBO__
19th ___ AUG

UGANDA WELCOMES BACK DR. DAIS__

Dr. Daisy's impassioned welcome by hundreds of national believers is heralded by a parade through the city, to alert the public about her upcoming Women's National·Congress.

THE SON OF GOD
JESUS CHRIST

Daisy negotiates contracts for printing huge quantities of the Osborn's books and tracts. Here, she inspects some of the tons of literature which she has arranged to be published prior to having it freighted to one of the Osborns' Mass Miracle Crusades for distribution to thousands of pastors, gospel workers, Bible students, and new converts.

Dr. Daisy clears another shipment of tons of gospel literature at a national border. After her dedicatory prayer (left), she distributes the treasured books to national pastors and church leaders, then takes time for special encouragement to the women.

Dr. Daisy believed that a successful teacher is an avid student. She says, "No one learns everything, but everyone can learn something. Once you have knowledge then you can share it to benefit someone else."

Dr. Daisy Osborn's private library contains rare treasures of knowledge to help womankind achieve the dignity of success.

Dr. Daisy and daughter, Senior Pastor LaDonna, dedicate a large stockpile of life-changing books plus audio and video Bible courses with manuals, all of which emphasize the biblical truths of redemption for women on the same level as for men.

Dr. Daisy assigns Bible Courses to delegates attending her World Conference at Tulsa from around the globe.

Whether at work in her private library, ministering to public audiences, or bringing healing to individuals, Dr. Daisy has always been a Jesus-woman of action, courageous, positive, dynamic and fruitful in ministry.

Chapter Twelve

Lessons For Living

MY DECISION TO title this book, *WHY?*, was influenced not only by the trauma I had experienced, but by the millions of disillusioned and despairing people who struggle in life with questions that destroy their faith and plunder their happiness.

Tragedy and trauma are a part of life but they must not have the last word—they must not triumph. Asking "WHY?" only exacerbates the confusion and deepens the wound.

As I penetrated the darkening shadows of my trauma, I had to quickly clamp the lid on my "WHYS?" I knew how deadly these questions can become when one is suffering grief.

Staying Alive

We have the power to absorb chaos, to manage loss, to refocus our view, and to continue our journey objectively, if we *will* to do so. Rather than to reject change, we can resolve to observe and ponder what is beautiful in our new scenery, and continue to live productively.

MAKING LOSS REDEMPTIVE

I have written this book partly because *I decided to survive — to keep living and loving.* I resolved that the painful loss of my dear and faithful companion in life must be made redemptive. Good must come from this heart-rending experience.

I felt that if I could express my calamity so that others could draw strength and healing from the lessons I had learned, that would give this experience redemptive value.

At first, I resolved to just bear the pain, and to say as little as possible. I saw no value in sharing my own dilemma.

But friends told me that the story of my own anguish was not the point. They believed that my reflections in this dark valley far transcended my own calamity and that they could bring infinite help, comfort, consolation and courage to others who may suffer loss of some kind.

That viewpoint gave purpose to writing my story. If people who have been wounded or demoralized by some kind of loss or devastation could be inspired to not give up on life but to rise and walk again—if the will to keep on living, productively, could be engendered in them—then

I could publish these personal experiences and lessons that I have learned, with some sense of having contributed good to others.

Options In Trauma

When trauma strikes, we have options. We can adjust our focus and *live*, or we can make our lives a misery to ourselves and to those around us. We are in charge of our own attitude. Our thoughts are subject to us.

If we are depressed and despondent, it is because of the thoughts we, ourselves, have chosen to ponder.

We can change our thoughts and paint a new picture, if we want to stay alive. I have learned to do that, and it is a lesson worth learning.

Self-Destruction Or Self-Renewal

After Daisy's homegoing, I found myself floundering in a dark valley of despairing loneliness. Although distraught and frustrated, I concluded that asking "WHY?" was negative and could become very destructive. It brought no healing and resolved no dilemma.

I was aware that a quest for the answer to why tragedy occurs often camouflages the deadly and insidious emotions of bitterness, resentment, exasperation, rancor, hostility, animosity, vengeance—all sentiments that produce a form of slow but sure self-destruction—and can even become suicidal.

There is a death that can happen *TO* us, which is tragic. But even more disastrous is another kind of death that happens *INSIDE* of us. One becomes a living dead person.

Venting Poignant Despair

The night of Daisy's demise, after her body had been rolled outside and then enclosed in the black hearse, the door had clanged shut. I stood there in anguish, separated from my lifetime sweetheart. I could never touch her warm body again.

The "WHYS?" roared inside of me. They were venting the poignant despair of separation. In panic, I felt incoherent. It was the kind of confusion that only exacerbates the suffering—the kind of questions that, if allowed to smolder, could become deadly and destructive.

It was enough to lose my beloved wife. I rationalized that I must not lose *myself, too.* Daisy would say "NO!" to my grieving. She would remind me that although her course was finished, mine was not. *There was divine purpose in my continuing to live.* I knew that I had to face the challenge of adjusting to a lifestyle without my companion. This was frightening to me but I to accept reality. My remaining life was *vital in God's plan.*

Refocusing Constructively

As my spirit was calmed by God's comforting presence, I could think with more clarity. By His grace, I could begin to absorb the grief and to assimilate the facts constructively. Then they could be refocused in the light of reality.

This trauma would always be a part of *what* and *who* I am, but I held the right of choice in how I would deal with it. It was my option to collapse in grief, or to *grow through it.*

I resolved that I would *grow,* that my being would be expanded by the pain I suffered, that I would be able to minister with greater compassion — maybe with more valid compassion.

While tears blurred my eyes, I could not see my way. I was entering a long and dark valley where the landscape was new, the scenery was unfamiliar, and the road was unknown.

But I told myself that this new vista *could* be beautiful, that the fresh scenery *could* be pleasant — even invigorating, if I could absorb my pain and see the good and the beauty in my new journey. God would be with me in His faithfulness, but it was up to me to summon the courage to continue living and to accept the changes that would be imposed.

The landscape of my past was familar. I did not want it to be changed. But I had to adjust.

Withdraw Or Lift The Torch

I had to be willing to release my treasured past and to reach for new meaning in my future. I was aware that life would be very different, but that it *could* be beautiful and full of purpose if I was willing to refocus my perspective and to reappraise my options in life.

I could choose to withdraw and *die*, or to keep lifting the gospel torch high in a darkened world, and *LIVE*. I knew that is what I must devote the rest of my life to.

The Bible prophet had said, *"I know the plans I have for you, says the Lord. They are plans for good and not for evil, to give you a future and a hope…When you pray, I will listen. You will find me when you seek me…"* Jer.29:11-13 LB

Life Is Too Precious To Squander

My Life was too valuable to be squandered in bereavement. Daisy and I had lived nearly fifty-four golden years together, giving ourselves to minister God's Love to multitudes. Masses of hurting humanity were still out there.

I could *choose* to continue ministering God's Love to millions in despair, loneliness, and spiritual desolation. I might even minister with greater compassion than before. I had tasted pain that I had never yet experienced.

In suffering one learns patience. In pain one learns tenderness. Maybe my love for people could be more authentic after having experienced this agony of grief.

"Acquainted With Grief"

I had come to realize more deeply than ever the sensitivity of our Lord for those who suffer. Is He not *"a man of sorrows, acquainted with grief?"* Isa.53:3 Paul said, *"He is touched with the feeling of our infirmities."* Heb.4:15

The Holy Spirit of God knows the groaning of those who sense despair and grief. To *"help our infirmities, the Spirit itself makes intercession for us with groaning which cannot be uttered."* Ro.8:26

God is concerned about the sorrows of His children. The Psalmist said, *"He has put our tears in a bottle."* Psa.56:8 He is aware of the hurts and heartbreaks of those who follow Him. He promises to *"wipe away all tears from our eyes."* Rev.7:17

In my despair, I remembered David asking, *"Why art thou cast down, O my soul?...HOPE thou in God."* Psa.42:5

In his times of suffering, Paul said that our Lord is *"The God of all comfort."* 2Co.1:3 *"He has loved us and given us everlasting consolation and good hope through grace, to comfort our hearts."* 2Thes.3:16 He speaks of *"the comfort of the scriptures."* Ro.15:4

David said, *"The law of the Lord is perfect, convert-*
ing the soul: the testimony of the Lord is sure, making
wise the simple. The statutes of the Lord are right, re-
joicing the heart: the commandment of the Lord is
pure, enlightening the eyes." Psa.19:7-8

I Had To Find The Light Again

As I drew strength from the scriptures, my eyes
were being *enlightened* in many ways. I began to
ponder and search for the beauty in my new vista
of life. Daisy was no longer touchable or ap-
proachable. I had to learn to live with *me,* and this
would be an unfamiliar experience. I did not
know *me* well enough to know I could learn to
enjoy life alone.

I knew I had to find the *Light* again. The shad-
owy night of despair had engulfed me. Daisy had
always been there to smile, to focus the best and
the brightest of every situation. I never in my life
heard her speak or suggest something negative.

Daisy believed in winning, in lifting people, in
triumphant success. She never was party to
doubt, indecision, uncertainty or hesitancy. She
was the light of my life and of our ministry.

But if I ran toward the dimming glow of Daisy's
dusk, I would never reach the light. I would only
self-destruct in my chase toward the setting sun.
The light would keep slipping beyond my reach.

The Route To A New Sunrise

The quickest and shortest route to the *Light* of a new day was to turn and to walk straight into the darkness. Although the bleak obscurity would be frightening, I would traverse it and arrive at the dawn of a fresh new sunrise. *I knew that I must traverse my dark night of despair in order to discover the golden light of my new day.*

I was aware that my life was hanging in suspense between the past that I loved *with Daisy*, and a future of loneliness *without her.* I did not want that future but I realized that I must accept it and that it was up to me to make it livable and pleasant.

My life as a husband was over. Now I was a *widower.* I hated the term. I was antagonized by the idea that I was no longer Daisy's husband.

Confused Bewilderment

As the torturous weeks passed, I would wear my wedding ring. On other occasions I would take it off and put it in a drawer. Then the next time I ministered, I would retrieve it and wear it again. I resented being *single.* I was only half there.

At times I would have the courage to minister without my wedding ring. I felt foolish, empty, confused. Waves of panic would overwhelm me.

There were periods of anger, disorientation, depression, pain, loneliness.

But I kept traversing the darkness toward a new sunrise.

Life Has The Final Word

I rationalized that *Life* and *Light* are more powerful than despair and darkness, more beautiful than despondency, more objective than remorse, more fruitful than sorrow. Daisy is in heaven because she embraced Christ and devoted her life to sharing Him with a hurting world.

Jesus had died so that suffering and bruised humanity could have hope and cure and peace. He had risen from the dead. *"It was not possible that He should be holden of death."* Ac.2:24 LIFE had the final word.

Jesus penetrated death and came out victorious *for us.* LIFE is the final victory for the believer — not Death. *LIGHT* is the final outcome — not Darkness.

Jesus said, *"Because I live, you shall live also."* Jn.14:19 His resurrection is our hope. It is our proof that Death and Darkness do not triumph. *Life* and *Light* are ours for the taking. Jesus promised that *"those who mourn shall be comforted."* Mt.5:4

Paul made it clear that God *"comforts us...so that we may be able to comfort [others] which are in any trouble, by the comfort wherewith we ourselves are comforted of God.* 2Co.1:4

He said, *"The Spirit of the Lord God is upon me, because He...has sent me to heal the brokenhearted."* Lu.4:18

Jesus lifted fallen people, restored broken lives, healed the sufferings and pain of those who were sick, comforted the heartbroken, consoled the despondent, stabilized the confused, was a companion and friend to the lonely. It is a great consolation to know that *Life* and *Light* have the last word for the Bible believer.

To Shrink Or To Expand

I learned quickly that the loss of a spouse or a loved one or a cherished friend is perhaps the most traumatic loss that one can experience. It either shrinks one's life, or *expands* it.

In discovering the awful pain of being separated from my beloved Daisy, I resolved that this experience would be a catalyst to *enlarge* my life, that it would not destroy me. As a Christian believer, I knew that I must *grow* through this grief, that I must *continue living and loving and ministering* in my hurting world.

Daisy Was My Best Half

The abrupt change in my perspective of life was more shocking and frightening than I can describe. We had lived as sweethearts for almost fifty-four years. We had married at ages seventeen and eighteen.

Daisy was my wonderful and loving wife, my patient companion and teammate in the Lord's work, my trusted colleague and associate in the ministry, my courageous and untiring co-worker in world evangelism, my special confidant and counselor in the affairs of life, my cherished and loving friend, my intimate sweetheart and *the* special lady in my life.

"Getting Over It"
Amputation Changes Everything

Now I was only a half-person. The best of me had been amputated. I had heard people say that one "gets over" these tragedies. Yes, I suppose, in a sense that must be true. But an amputation *forces* traumatic changes.

Daisy's eldest brother, Bud, is a *double-amputee*. At age seventeen, his right arm was shot off. At age fifty, his left arm was removed following a traffic accident.

I suppose one could say that Bud "got over it." He has become remarkably adept using two prostheses to dress, to eat, to bathe, to work, to drive. He even restores the most delicate of antiques, paintings, porcelains.

Bud is a daily challenge to all who know him. He is positive and uplifting, never self-consoling. I have watched him *grow* through his adversity. His attitude has been a great help to me.

THE RESULTS ARE PERMANENT

So one could say that Bud "got over it." But the results are permanent. The impact has been incalculable. And the consequences are cumulative.

Everything that Bud does is a reminder that he is a double amputee. Bathing, dressing, eating, lying in bed, and whatever he does, his lifestyle has been changed. Many gratifications, actions and duties that he once enjoyed or performed as a normal part of life are now set aside.

He has adapted himself to his new agenda. One could say that Bud has "gotten over it." Yes, but *Bud will use hooks for the rest of his life.*

DRASTIC CHANGES

I am told that I will "get over" Daisy's demise. Yes, as time goes on, I suppose that I'll learn to get along "on crutches". And, who knows, I may even learn to derive support from "artificial limbs"...*but my life will never be the same.* It is drastically changed. What are my options? I am determined to make the best of life—even being handicapped as I now am. My world needs me, *even if I am functioning with some awkwardness.*

My vista is altered now. A dam has been broken. Devastation has swept over my landscape. It's all different now. So much that was beautiful is gone.

I no longer have a future *with Daisy*. From here on, *I am a widower*. I do not want to be a widower. I hate being a widower, but *I am a widower*. I am not Daisy's husband any more. I am not married now. I am *single*. I hate that term too. I am *alone*. I hate being alone. My aloneness is frustrating—frightening to me.

The Music In Life

I have a tape player on my kitchen countertop. A great gospel pianist came to my house and played my piano for me. I recorded his playing. I love the piano. I play his tape while I prepare and eat my breakfast and lunch. I need music. I must have music. *I cannot permit the music in my spirit to die*. Life must include the wonder of music.

My Nine Foot Grand Piano

We have always had a piano in our home. But I decided to buy myself a bigger, nicer one. So I put on a search and bought a nearly new nine-foot Baldwin concert grand. I love to play the piano. It provides an emotional outlet for me. It releases my tensions. I cannot explain why but music is a great consolation to me.

Playing the piano helps me when I am writing. If I find myself in a stall-out for words or thoughts, I play the piano. Everything becomes free again. There is liberation in music.

I am learning to see more and more beauty along my new journey. I expect good things—beautiful things, albeit *different* things. Waves of resentment lambaste me at times because I do not want this new, lonely life. I want life like it was before with my companion and sweetheart. But that part of my life is over.

Coming To Grips With Change

Groping along with my best half amputated, I have to face many limitations that I did not experience while Daisy was with me. Like a physically disabled person, I resent my limitations, but I must come to grips with them.

Yes, with my choice-power and resolve to look for what is good, life is still beautiful, but it is *very different*. I have decided to adapt where necessary because my life—even *alone*, has value.

The truths that I know, can help heal a hurting world. I must continue to disseminate that healing influence. I am a Bible believer. God is at work in me. I am His messenger, His ambassador, His representative. What I know can lift and restore hurting human persons. So...*I must continue to LIVE.*

I struggle to avoid *limiting my expectations.* Without Daisy, so much has changed. But I remind myself that God is the same. It is His strength that bears me up. So I resist the demeaning gloom of *limited* expectations.

Paul's words comfort me. He counseled, *"This one thing I do, forgetting those things which are behind, and reaching forth unto those things which are before, I press toward the mark for the prize of the high calling of God in Christ Jesus."* Phi.3:13-14 That helps me. That is what I am doing.

Releasing The Good As Well As The Bad

Daisy always said that we must constantly *release the past — the good times as well as the bad ones.* I suppose that in coming to the end of ourselves, we can discover a fresh relationship with God.

My greatest difficulty has been in coming to grips with a new identity. It has been repulsive to me. I didn't want another selfhood. Daisy and I were always *T.L. & Daisy.* Now I am...*T.L.* – a half-person. My equilibrium seems to be gone. I feel off-balance. Surges of bitterness swell within me. I've been tempted to become a recluse.

A New Identity

I've fought a desperate struggle in coming to grips with *me* being alone. Life had always been *we.* Things had been *ours.* Now it is *me.* Things have become *mine.* I hate the idea of something being *mine.* Daisy and I had been partners in everything. Without her, the camaraderie that I had known is gone. The pendulum of my life has swung between acceptance or rejection, resentment or a new commitment, withdrawing into the past or reaching into the future, grief and bitterness for what I have lost or joy and gratitude for all that remains.

Growing Through Change

Do I want Daisy back? Then, someday we would face death and separation *again.* Do I want to repeat the death process? I had to face the darkness. One cannot keep things as they *were.* Life means change. Change means growth. So I realized that I must *grow through this change.* But I did not want to grow. I wanted to keep things as they had been.

Miracles - Temporary Solutions

The unconquered enemy is *Death.* No supernatural wonder can save us from it. Miracles, as much as I believe in them, are *temporary solutions.* Some of the people who have received the greatest miracles we ever witnessed are now dead.

Juan Santos dragged on the ground for sixteen years, having been shot through his spine and left dead from his waist down. He was miraculously healed in one of our crusades. He traveled wherever he could to give public testimony of the wondrous miracle that he had received. But Juan Santos grew old *and he died.*

The Moslem Beggar

Karimu, a Moslem beggar, crawled on the ground for thirty years. He came to our crusade and was miraculously healed. The whole city knew him and hundreds of people gave their lives to Christ because of the influence of his miracle and change of life. Daisy gave him a new Christian name, Cornelius. He journeyed all over Nigeria witnessing for Jesus Christ who had healed him. But today, *Cornelius is dead.*

The Leper Woman

Miriam Gare was a leper. Her hands and feet were gone. She crawled to our meeting and huddled under the cover of a tree to hear the gospel. Jesus passed her way and healed her. Her flesh became clean.

The Provincial Commissioner wrote to tell us that the whole Province believed in God now because of the miraculous healing of this noted leper. She became a faithful member of the church pastored by Rev. Silas Owiti and her witness caused many people to believe on Jesus Christ. But in later years, *Miriam died.* Today she is in heaven.

Jesus Raised Lazarus From The Dead Today He Is Dead Again

Jesus healed the blind, the deaf, the lame and the insane. He even raised Lazarus from the dead. But those beautiful people *are all deceased today — including Lazarus* whom he brought back from the corruption of death.

Miracles are just *temporary answers*. The Bible says, *"It is appointed unto [people] once to die."* *Heb.9:27* My beloved Daisy's time came and *she died*. I was left alone in the same way that millions of spouses had been before me.

Reappraising The New Landscape

It was time to refocus my life, to reappraise the value of living, to reassess the privilege of being alive in this world where so many hurting people need the power of God's healing Love.

I began recalculating the potential of *Life with God* amidst people who hurt. I was chosen by Him to be a minister and a witness of Jesus Christ and a communicator of His grace and healing. *"I had not chosen Him, but He had chosen me, and had ordained me, that I should go and bring forth fruit..."* *Jn.15:16* That was a positive mission. That expressed life with purpose — with meaning. That offered hope and reason for living. I was part of God's big plan. Destiny was at work in me. I was involved with *The Master*. I was *not* alone.

THERE IS PURPOSE IN LIFE WITH God

I felt what Paul must have felt when the Lord Jesus said to him, *"Rise and stand upon your feet: for I have appeared unto you for this purpose, to make you a minister and a witness..."*

He was told, *"I am sending you to the [non-Christians], to open their eyes, and to turn them from darkness to light, and from the power of Satan unto God, that they may receive the forgiveness of sins, and inheritance among them which are sanctified by faith that is in me."* Ac.26:16-18

Jesus and His purpose had been the guiding light, the motivating factor for Daisy and me in our half-century of ministry together. That would continue to be *my* guiding light. I would always focus on the unreached millions, doing all within my means to reach them with the gospel.

His Purpose Is Unchanged

Nothing about Jesus and His promises had changed. Nothing about the needs of our hurting world was different. Only *I had been changed.* I had suffered an amputation. I was struggling with the awkwardness of some "clumsy prostheses." But I was alive. I could navigate. I had a voice to speak, eyes to see, ears to hear, and arms to embrace. My heart was full. My mind was alive. I burned with His love and compassion for needy people — maybe more than ever.

I was refocusing my life, my scenery, my prospects. The landscape was different, but there was beauty if I *took time to smell the roses.* Jesus was my center. God was my hope, my courage, my help, my strong tower. *Ps.61:3; Pr.18:10* Though I was alone, *"He was the strength of my life" Psa.27:1* — and He was *sufficient.* I could continue. Life could be beautiful and productive. I could keep on doing what He had called and ordained me to do: *"To go and to bear fruit." Jn.15:16* That would be worth living for.

Being Lifted By Lifting Others

I would receive healing by bringing healing to others. My loneliness would dissipate by introducing Jesus to despairing people as their new friend. The pain of my loss would subside as God's grace assuaged the pain of others through my ministry. I could, I would hoist my shoulders and press on with maybe a greater depth of faith, love, hope, and joy than I had known before.

The Defining Moment
The Reexamination

The loss that I had suffered had been a defining moment. It had brought me to a total reappraisal of life. It impelled me toward a reexamination of assets that *remained.* It forced me to ask penetrating questions. What really counted? What mattered in the final analysis? What did I really believe? What kind of person was T.L. Osborn? Did he really care for hurting people? A reappraisal of my own person, will, faith, and purpose was taking place.

Choice For Survival
Hues Of A Fresh Dawn

My choice-power had been my stabilizer. Rather than to bemoan forever my loss, I resolved to assess the abundance that remained in my life. I had been willing to face my dark night of devastating grief, to walk straight into it, and to traverse the haunting shadows of bereavement.

Because of my choice for survival, I was seeing the hopeful hues of a fresh dawn. The sunlight would shine again. A new day was being born. I had made the right choice—a choice to live and not die, to expand and not shrink, to march on and not recoil, to keep reaching out to my hurting world and not to retreat in wasteful bereavement. *LIFE was having the last word for me.*

New Panorama Of Life

I had not been able to prevent the tragedy that had occurred. But I *had* been able to refocus my attitude and to pick up my brush and begin to paint a new panorama of life.

The power of choice was my control center. Walking into the dark was my quickest route to a new sunrise. I had set myself to reach a new dawn. I had run toward the *east* rather than weakening myself by chasing the *west*ward memories of a day that had past and was gone.

Light And Life Triumphant

I had grown through my trauma. God's grace and His *Life* had triumphed.

I awake each morning *to LIVE.* I still yearn—my body and my person ache—for Daisy. My psyche is still programmed to share life and plans and ideas and concepts and news with her. I hear of things and instinctively want to share them with her, but she is no longer there. That part of my life is gone. I am learning to cope with my new lifestyle. It is very different. But I am determined to find all of the beauty that I can discern in my journey.

The Cloud Of Witnesses

The heritage of those who have died in the faith holds before me a triumphant standard to live by. Like all believers, I will pass from this life some day. But while I am alive in this world, I re-solve—I choose—to live joyfully, productively, triumphantly.

"I am compassed about by a great cloud of wit-nesses" Heb.12:1 who have, like Paul the apostle— and like Daisy, *"fought a good fight, finished their course, kept the faith: and there is laid up for them a*

crown...*which the Lord, the righteous judge, shall give to them at that day."* 2Tim.4:7-8

Those committed men and women lived their lives nobly and died in the faith. They were the kind of people I wanted to emulate. Paul said to *"be followers of those who through faith and patience inherit the promises."* Heb.6:12 Daisy was one of those noble women who had *"held the beginning of her confidence steadfast unto the end."* Heb.3:13

The heritage of this *"cloud of witnesses"* motivates me to give my best in service to humanity. The standard and conduct of life that they have lived inspires me to *keep living* and to *keep ministering* God's love in our hurting world.

Their Legacy Motivates Me

Their *record* motivates me. Their *poetry* inspires me. Their *songs* lift my spirit. Their *music* refreshes my being. Their *words* give me faith. Their *works* challenge me. Their *metaphors* and *images* help me to refocus my new horizon. Their *convictions* help me to remember the things that really matter in life.

Millions of those who have predeceased me have endured loss as great and more excruciating than what I have experienced.

"Some of them were tortured, not accepting deliverance; that they might obtain a better resurrection: Others had trial of cruel mockings and scourgings,

suffering bonds and imprisonment: They were stoned, sawn asunder, tempted, slain with the sword: they wandered about in sheepskins and goatskins; being destitute, afflicted, tormented; (Of whom the world was not worthy:) they wandered in deserts, and in mountains, and in dens and caves of the earth. And these all, having obtained a good report through faith, received not the promise: God having provided some better thing…" Heb.11:35-40

No wonder the writer added: *"Since we are compassed about with so great a cloud of witnesses, let us …run with patience the race that is set before us, LOOKING UNTO JESUS the author and finisher of our faith; who for the joy that was set before Him endured the cross, despising the shame, and is set down at the right hand of the throne of God. For CONSIDER HIM…lest ye be wearied and faint in your minds."* Heb.12:1-3

Passing The Torch To Others

I am resolved that my remaining life shall be a legacy of faith for those who follow me. Others have influenced and inspired me — like Daisy has, with her sun-filled life and example. Now it is my turn to influence and inspire those who may need to draw strength from my example.

Tragedy, trauma, devasting and demoralizing loss occurs in life. It comes in many forms. But we can survive if we *will* to live. *We have a choice.*

Giving Dignity To Existence

No one is an island. Our lives are intertwined. We are part of each other. We mark people by our example—for better or for...not-so-good. Paul said, *"I am a debtor"* Rom.1:14 to the people in my world. *"We are not our own; we are bought with a price."* 1Co.6:20 We are *"members of Christ,"* 1Co.6:15 and *"of one another."* Eph.4:25 I belong to God's family and am part of His plan. I count. That gives dignity to life and nobility to living.

Yes, my choice power is my control center. After the storm has swept past, then the tragic loss is realized. But a new inventory is made. Whatever remains is appraised and, with those precious remnants, the journey of life is resumed. It is starkly different, but it is *life*, and it must go on, and the sun will rise again. No one has license to *quit on living.*

A Choice To Love Again

I made another crucial discovery—there was another option before me. It was *a choice to LOVE again.* At my age of seventy-four, that choice was not to love another spouse. That part of my life was over. Daisy fulfilled me. I could ask for no more. Almost fifty-four years of life with her as sweethearts, was an abundant portion. I could be satisfied.

But I knew that I must *choose to LOVE again* — to love people, to love a hurting world, to love the ministry, to love crusading and conducting seminars, to love teaching and preaching and healing the sick and suffering. Yes, I made that choice without hesitation. *I chose to LOVE again.*

CHAPTER THIRTEEN

DAISY GOES HOME

"HIGHER DIMENSIONS" TRIBUTE

DR. DAISY MARIE Washburn Osborn was surrounded by her husband T.L., daughter La-Donna Osborn Nickerson, and two grandchildren—LaDonna's daughters, LaVona and Daneesa, the night that she expired. Dr. T.L. held her in his arms as she slipped into eternity at 2:53 a.m. Saturday, May 27, 1995.

Daisy had summoned the family, requesting that they advise friends not to pray for her restoration. She was ready to go home. Three times she had seen an angel come into the room and sit on a golden couch (which only she saw), as though waiting to escort her through the veil of mortality into God's presence.

Associate Pastor Chyanna Anthony was visiting the family when Daisy made this request. She was profoundly impressed, not that Daisy spoke in a matter-of-fact tone, but that *"there was no spirit of death in the room."*

Senior Pastor LaDonna described the atmosphere around Daisy during her last week as being
charged with an overwhelming spirit of peace—
in which no one could weep. The coronation of a
great woman of God was imminent.

Well known as the First Lady of Evangelism,
Dr. Daisy, along with her husband, T.L., are said
to have preached face to face to more unevangelized people than any couple in history. Three
years ago, they spent their 50th wedding anniver-
sary in India, the nation that motivated their
massive healing crusade ministry that had expanded to seventy-three nations, with audiences
numbering from 25,000 to 300,000 per meeting.

Daisy, with T.L., was a great humanitarian—
responsible for taking truckloads of medical
supplies into places like East Africa, working
with orphanages, and assisting underdeveloped
countries in many ways. They were regularly received by Heads of State and other high government officials.

A great crusader for women's equality in
Christ, Dr. Daisy's example in ministry and her
teaching were globally influential in upgrading
the status of women in the Church. She was the
first woman to preach in some nations.

Dr. Margaret Idahosa of Nigeria said, *"Wherever
in the world there is something going on for women in*

God's work, if you trace it, you will find Mama Daisy's influence."

Mama Daisy was an advisor to many international leaders in the Church. The ministries and world outreaches of her and T.L. resulted in many thousands of new churches being established in previously unevangelized areas—hundreds of which are pastored by women in nations that traditionally demean women and forbid them from leadership positions.

Dr. Daisy was born on September 23, 1924, in Merced, California—the tenth of eleven children. She was born again at the age of twelve. In 1942, at the age of seventeen, she married Tommy Lee (T.L.) Osborn, a young evangelist from Oklahoma. (He had helped Oral Roberts in street meetings in their early years, playing his accordian with Oral who played his guitar and sang.)

Daisy and T.L. were married on Easter Sunday and immediately went into full time ministry. They had four children, three of whom predeceased Daisy.

In 1983, Daisy Washburn Osborn was awarded an Honorary Doctor of Letters degree by Bethel Christian College in California, and an Honorary Doctor of Theology degree by Zoe College in Florida. She is listed in the *International Directory of Distinguished Leadership*, the *International Register of Profiles*, *Who's Who of American Women*,

Who's Who in Women's Ministry, and the *World Who's Who of Women.*

Daughter LaDonna, Senior Pastor-Overseer of *International Gospel Center,* officiated at the memorial celebration of her mother's homegoing.

The pallbearers, at the request of Dr. Daisy, were eight female, ordained, ministers of the gospel representing Malaysia, India, Africa, Kenya, France and the United States. They refused to allow the casket to be transported to the hearse on the portable base. One of the women was heard to say, *"As pallbearers, we want to carry it all the way."*

According to the coroner's report, death was due to respiratory infection that contributed to congestive heart failure.

Pastor LaDonna quoted her father: *"Anytime or any place that Daisy is not with me, I always preach some for her, and I will continue to do that."* He is currently working on their *24-Volume Faith Library and Anthology of Their World Ministries* that will be placed in select Bible Schools and institutions of higher learning in nations abroad, to serve as a witness to coming generations that *"Jesus Christ is the same yesterday, today and forever."* Heb.13:8

Chapter Fourteen

A Torch Held High

Salute By Sue Hyatt - August 26, 1995

> Gal. 2:20. "I have been crucified with Christ; it is no longer I who live, but Christ lives in me; and the life which I now live, I live by the faith of the Son of God, who loved me and gave Himself for me."

Daisy didn't die on Saturday;
Daisy died a long time ago.

For years, like Paul,
Daisy lived no longer,
So Christ lived big in her.

That is why we were drawn to her.
That is why we loved her so.

She helped us see better
When the path seemed dark.
She helped us feel warm
When the world seemed cold.

She was for us a torch
Burning brightly,
Sustained and held high
In God's Mighty Hand.

She was for us a torch, indeed,
Soaked in the Oil of God's Spirit
Ablaze with the Fire of the Holy One.

But she was human like us, you see,
So her flesh was, at last, consumed,
And Daisy died
As all of us must one day.

But while we live,
Let us also die as Daisy did
And be torches held high,
Giving light and giving warmth.

Daisy has not passed a torch on
To you and me;
Daisy had no torch to pass!

Does that surprise you?
No, Daisy had no torch for us to grasp.
Daisy was herself *A Torch Held High*!

Do you yet understand?
We too are torches
Meant to burn brightly
In the night, in the cold.

That is our destiny,
Our dream, our delight.

But how, I asked, can I bring
Warmth and light as Daisy did?
I did not understand.

So I asked,
"Daisy, what is it about you?
I too desire to obey our Lord's command,
But I feel useless, helpless, insignificant!

I too aspire to bring healing, hope, and life,
But I feel inadequate, afraid, unsure."

And she replied, *"Go and do likewise!"*
That was all. And she walked away.

What did she mean?
Surely she would show me
what, and when, and where, and how?
Surely she would give me five steps to follow,
Ten principles to use,
One key that would unlock it all!

So I mused and watched and realized;
Daisy was human like us all,
But one thing was different:

Daisy had died a long time ago.
Her life was her Lord's;
Her light, not her own.

Yes, Daisy had died a long time ago,
And she was a torch soaked in the Oil,
Ablaze with the Fire, held high
by God's Mighty Hand.

And that is what drew us.
But we did not understand
why she would not tell us what to do.

She would only say,
"Pray. Listen and pray."
She knew there was no rigid pattern,
No religious rule worthwhile.

She talked to God
And listened for His wisdom,
Then admonished us to do the same.
That is what she meant when she said to me,
"Go and do likewise."

So Daisy has not passed a torch to you, to me.
Daisy, was herself a torch, you see.
Not a small torch,
Not a flickering torch
As we so often seem to be!

What made her light intense?
What made her warmth contagious?
I have thought. I have prayed.
And like paint on a barren canvas,
Her portrait appears
In bold splashes and gentle strokes
Of Compassion,
Of Commitment,
Of Courage.

COMPASSION constrained her.
COMMITMENT sustained her.
And COURAGE compelled her never to quit.

Yes, Compassion constrained her
To meet human need.

Daisy was smart,
Smart enough to know
That needs always exceeded her capacity;
Smart enough to lean completely on God
Who is always bigger than human need

So she became a torch of light and warmth
for you, for me, for millions.

Yes, *Commitment* sustained her
In difficulty, in sorrow, in pain.

Daisy was smart,
Smart enough to do what she *had* to do,
Not what she *wanted* to do;
Smart enough to do what compassion required,
Not what comfort and convenience craved.

It was not easy, It was not glamorous;
Commitment never is.

Yes, *Courage* compelled her
In spite of biased and unlettered resistance.

Daisy was smart,
Smart enough to believe
That God Who had called her
Was big enough to cause the seed to grow.

Yes, we were inspired by her courage.
But did we realize it was born of compassion?
And did we understand
The cost of her commitment?

Courage motivated by compassion
And sustained by commitment
Confronts all resistance,
And with Godly wisdom
Accomplishes His mission.

(Well done, Daisy!
Thou good and faithful servant.
Enter into the rest of the Lord.)

And that is what we saw.
That is what we felt.
That is what drew us.

There will never be another Daisy.
And there will never be another *You*.

Chapter Fifteen

"But Mama Did!"

LaDonna's 21-Verse Salute To Her Mother

1. They say, "Women cannot publicly preach the gospel with power."
    But Mama did!

2. They say, "Women cannot pastor churches."
    But Mama did!

3. They say, "Women cannot baptize new converts in water."
    But Mama did!

4. They say, "Women cannot administer the Holy Communion to the Body of Christ."
    But Mama did.

5. They say, "Women cannot unite couples in Holy Matrimony."
    But Mama did.

6. They say, "Women cannot license or ordain people for gospel ministry."
    But Mama did.

7. They say, "Women cannot hold offices of authority in the Church."
    But Mama did.

8.   They say, "Women cannot give authoritative leadership in Christian ministry."
But Mama did.

9.   They say, "Women cannot serve the Church in the office of an apostle."
But Mama did.

10.   They say, "Women cannot use their voices to teach or preach in the Church."
But Mama did.

11.   They say, "Women cannot cast out devils and minister to the sick if a man is present to do it."
But Mama did.

12.   They say, "Married women cannot hear directly from God apart from their husbands."
But Mama did.

13.   They say, "Women cannot be good wives and mothers and be active in public ministry."
But Mama did.

14.   They say, "Mothers cannot travel with their children and give them a good education."
But Mama did.

15.   They say, "Women should not use their maiden names."
But Mama did.

16.   They say, "Wives cannot serve in ministry on an equal basis with their husbands."
But Mama did.

17.   They say, "Women in leadership do not have good relationships with daughters and with other women."
But Mama did.

18.   They say, "Successful women do not share the spotlight with other women."
But Mama did.

19.   They say, "Women cannot help being emotional or avoid being deceived."
But Mama did.

20.   They say, "Women cannot fully represent Jesus in life and in ministry."
But Mama did.

21.   They say, "Women do not leave seed as their spiritual legacy to their world."
But Mama did.

ഔ

CHAPTER SIXTEEN

IN THY PRESENCE
IS FULNESS OF JOY
(PSALM 16:11)
Biographical Brief

DAISY MARIE WASHBURN Osborn was born September 23, 1924. She was one of eleven children born to Christopher Columbus Washburn and Clara Irene Oates Washburn. Her mother was killed in an auto-train accident in 1932. Daisy became a ward of the State of California and her eldest sister, Ruby Parsley became her legal guardian and raised her.

In 1942, Daisy married Tommy Lee (T.L.) Osborn, an evangelist from Oklahoma. They conducted church revivals until 1944 when they established and pastored a new church, *Montavilla Tabernacle*, in Portland, Oregon.

Daisy and T.L. were appointed as missionaries to India in 1945 and became world missionary evangelists in 1948.

In 1949 Daisy co-founded, with her husband, a world missionary church organization, *Voice of Faith Ministry, Inc.* (later amended to *Osborn Evangelistic Ass'n*, then *Osborn Foundation*, and finally *OSFO International*).

Mother & Teammate In World Evangelism

Daisy Osborn was the mother of four children, Marie LaVon (deceased in 1943), Tommy Lee, Jr., (deceased in 1979), LaDonna Carol Osborn, Senior Pastor Overseer of *International Gospel Center* at Tulsa, Oklahoma, and Mary Elizabeth (deceased in 1951).

She had six grandchildren (four girls and two boys) and thirteen great grandchildren (nine boys and four girls).

Daisy was married to T.L. for over fifty-three years. They shared their worldwide gospel ministry in a unique and practical way.

From their early marriage, they ministered side by side as teammates. She not only was the Chief Executive Officer of their world organization, but carried her equal share of their writing, filming, recording, preaching, and teaching ministries. Daisy Osborn probably ministered, face-to-face, to more millions of people, in more nations, than any other woman who ever lived. After thirty-five years in ministry, the Lord gave Daisy a special revelation concerning women in the Church.

Divine Visitation

In 1947, the Lord visited Daisy and offered her the choice of staying home to raise her children, or of going to the world to teach and preach the gospel. She chose to go. Some years later, Christ appeared to her from a mountaintop of light, walking toward her as He spoke these words, *"Daisy, preach the gospel to women."* As the apostle Paul, she could say, *"I was not disobedient unto the heavenly vision."* Acts 22:19

Schoolteacher, Preacher, Linguist, Conference Speaker

For over nine years, she taught her children, Tommy and LaDonna, under the *Calvert School System* used internationally by USA State Department personnel. She later wrote and published an autobiographical story entitled, *"I Chose To Go."*

She proclaimed the gospel in churches, auditoriums, ballrooms, theaters, tents, on racetracks and ball fields, in stadiums, and out on open parks or terrains in seventy-four different nations. She spoke and ministered in three languages, English, Spanish and French.

Daisy conducted Women's Seminars and Conferences across the globe. It was common for five to seven thousand women to attend her events.

INTERNATIONAL AUTHOR

She authored five major books: *The Woman Believer, Five Choices For Women Who Win, Women andSelf-Esteem, Woman Without Limits, and New Life for Women*. Also Daisy wrote almost thirty other smaller books and dozens of major articles for the Osborns' international magazine, *Faith Digest*, mailed monthly to over a hundred nations.

CINEMATOGRAPHER

In 1954, during the Osborn Campaign in Djakarta, Java, Daisy recorded the wonders of the meetings on film. In addition to directing the crusade, she photographed the multitudes and the miracles. Later, she and her husband, with the expertise and musical score of Lonnie Rex, produced the docu-miracle film, *Java Harvest*.

That film made such an impression wherever it was shown that it motivated Daisy to record subsequent crusades. The Osborns' repertoire of docu-miracle films include: *Java Harvest, Black Gold, The Ghanaian, The Holland Wonder, Athens of India, Filipino Passion, Luzon Reaper, The Unlimited God, Miracle Worker, Healer of Trinidad, Nakuru Crusade*, plus nine videos of their great India Crusade.

Those docu-miracle films have been translated and produced in sixty-seven major languages of the world. Many hundreds of copies of them (on 16 mm film and on all video formats) are constantly circulated throughout the world. They have motivated an international reappraisal of Christian concepts for world missions and international evangelism.

Daisy's teaching and preaching on video and audio cassettes, are affecting women, as well as men, around the world. Books and gospel tracts authored by T.L. and Daisy are published in 132 languages.

Minister Of Love To Millions

Daisy has brought hope and faith to millions of women throughout the world. She conducted the first massive Women's Congress in the history of India, where thousands of women congregated daily under a hot *shamina* (flat tent) in 110° Fahrenheit heat, to hear her teach concerning their identity, dignity, destiny and equality in God's redemptive plan. Hundreds of those women have become active in gospel ministries.

National Women's Conferences

In Uganda, the *Conference Arena* of the United Nations of Africa was packed with thousands of women twice daily, to attend Dr. Daisy Osborn's Pan-African Women's Congress. Hundreds of

those women have become full time gospel ministers, pastors, churchbuilders, evangelists, and
itinerant village preachers.

In Bogota, Colombia, Daisy's Pan-American
Women's Conference, conducted in the large
Sports Arena, was attended by three to six thousand women — the largest Christian women's conference in South American history.

Daisy's enlightening and biblical teaching has
inspired women around the world to discover
their unlimited scope of ministry as followers of
Jesus Christ.

In her books and audio-courses, she reveals Bible truths that have inspired and motivated tens
of thousands of women to find within themselves
those special gifts and talents which, when linked
to God's perfect design, produce the fruits of
fulfillment, self-esteem and true happiness.

IdentitY In RedEmption
InternAtionAl DiplomAt

Daisy Osborn's life and ministry have helped
multitudes to discover that in Christ there is
equality; that every true believer shares the same
relationship with Him — the same identity, the
same ministry, the same calling, the same
anointing — regardless of race, gender, color or
nationality.

As Crusade Director for the Osborn Crusades, Daisy became an international diplomat with *entrée* into the highest circles of government. She numbered among her personal friends, kings and presidents, state and local dignitaries.

National Sons & Daughters Of The Soil

In 1953, Daisy and her husband conceived a world missionary plan of assisting trained and qualified national sons and daughters-of-the-soil who would go as missionaries to tribes, villages, towns and areas unreached by the gospel. From its inception, Daisy supervised this broad evangelism program, making the decision on each national minister to be assisted.

They fully sponsored over 30,000 national missionaries who have evangelized and established new pioneer churches in more than 136,000 different areas of the world, through the field supervision of over 200 foreign and national missionary church organizations. For many years, by diligently keeping her finger on the pulse of the program, Dr. Daisy was able to register an average establishment of over one new self-supporting church per day—more than four hundred per year.

Managing The Transport Of Tools For Evangelism Worldwide

Throughout the decades of the Osborns' international evangelism ministries, Dr. Daisy managed and negotiated innumerable airlifts and surface shipments of hundreds of tons of literature, tools for evangelism, mobile evangelism vehicles, and other equipment to missionary and national church agencies around the world.

One shipment into East Africa required the leasing of a Boeing 747 jet airplane to transport more than a hundred tons of equipment and literature to the continent for church workers from seven different nations.

A huge airlift into Nigeria required Daisy's personal negotiation with the *National Army* to station soldiers at the Lagos airport to guard the unloading of the materiel and to accompany its overland transport to the location of distribution.

Once, Daisy flew to the opposite side of the world to meet and negotiate with a Head of State, achieving the cancellation of a customs assessment of more than $125,000 on an Osborn airlift of evangelism equipment. The President allowed it to enter the nation free of duty.

Director Of Vast Global Ministries

For decades, the daily supervision and direction of the vast global ministries of the Osborns' world ministry rested upon Daisy as the association's CEO.

Decisions that committed hundreds of thousands of missionary dollars in worldwide strategic projects, affecting millions of souls for Christ, have been made by Daisy's experienced and seasoned judgment.

Lady Of Evangelism

This intrepid *Lady of Evangelism* personally conducted difficult language workshops in such far-flung areas as Viet Nam, Papua New Guinea, Sri Lanka, and other areas worldwide where the Osborns' sermon tapes and docu-miracle films have been translated into 67 languages.

Her daily worldwide correspondence ministry with government heads and national church leaders has been extensive.

Her knowledge of French and Spanish has facilitated her in effective ministry and management of evangelism programs, not only in Latin America, Spain and France, but in dozens of other nations where those major languages are spoken.

Who's Who International

Daisy served as international advisor and was lifetime patron of *Christian Women's College;* a member of the board of regents at *Bethel Christian College* and is listed in *The International Directory of*

Distinguished Leadership, The International Register of Profiles, Who's Who of American Women, Who's Who in Women's Ministry, Who's Who in Religion, and *The World Who's Who of Women.* She held an L.H.D. (honorary) bestowed by *Bethel Christian College,* Riverside, California; and a D.D. (honorary), conferred by *Zoe College,* Jacksonville, Florida.

Soulwinner, Administrator Kingdom Business Ambassador

Her more than five decades of active ministry in seventy-four nations, as author, radio minister, national and international preacher, conference and seminar speaker, businesswoman, great grandmother, grandmother, mother, wife, soulwinner, teacher, and world ambassadress for Christ—plus her administrative, diplomatic and business roles in the Osborn organization's world ministries, have distinguished Daisy Marie Washburn Osborn as one of God's very special women and have numbered her among the most outstanding and experienced female ministers of the Church of Jesus Christ in her generation.

Triumphant Transition

Daisy Marie Washburn Osborn transcended her mortality to be forever with her Lord on May 27, 1995.

Like the Bible Psalmist David, *"After [Daisy] had served her own generation by the will of God, she fell asleep, and was laid with her foreparents..."* Acts 13:36

"I Have Set The Lord Always Before Me"

Her testimony was, *"Thou art my hope, O Lord God: Thou art my trust from my youth."* Psa.71:5 Her witness: *"I have set the Lord always before me: because He is at my right hand, I shall not be moved. Therefore, my heart is glad, and my glory rejoiceth: my flesh also shall rest in hope ... In Thy presence is fulness of joy; at Thy right hand there are pleasures for evermore."* Psa. 16:8-9,11 *"Being justified by His grace, I have been made an heir according to the hope of eternal life."* Titus 3:7

Daisy's Seed Runs With The Message

Like her foremother Sarah, Daisy *"received strength to conceive [spiritual] seed. Therefore sprang there...so many [handmaidens, daughters upon whom the Spirit of the Lord has been poured out* Acts 2:17-18*] as the stars of the sky in multitude, and as the sand which is by the sea shore innumerable."* Heb.11:11-12